Trevor Griffiths read English Literature and Language at Manchester University and taught for eight years before becoming a Further Education Officer for the BBC in Leeds. During this time he edited a series of publications for the Workers' Northern Publishing Association and wrote a number of plays, including *Occupations*. In 1972 he left the BBC to write full-time and has since written widely for film, theatre and television.

THE GULF
BETWEEN US
or
THE TRUTH
AND OTHER
FICTIONS

TREVOR GRIFFITHS

faber and faber
LONDON · BOSTON

First published in 1992
by Faber and Faber Limited
3 Queen Square London WCIN 3AU

Photoset by Parker Typesetting Service, Leicester
Printed in England by Clays Ltd, St Ives plc

Introduction © The West Yorkshire Playhouse, 1992
© Commonty Productions Ltd, 1992

Trevor Griffiths is hereby identified as author of this work in accordance with
Section 77 of the Copyright, Designs and Patents Act 1988

A CIP record for this book is available from the British Library

ISBN 0-571-16728-4

INTRODUCTION
Trevor Griffiths talks to the West Yorkshire Playhouse

How did you come to write The Gulf between Us?

I'd started working on an idea with Paul Slack and Dave Hill some time before Christmas 1990 and the idea involved building a wall in real time, on stage, every night. Originally I wasn't involved as a writer, I was just there as a sort of ideas man and a possible director for this project – it interested me, and the idea of creating a company to do new work interested me.

While we were discussing this, talking through these ideas, the deadline was set for the Gulf War. So out of the corner of my eye I was always watching the geopolitical scene and sensing with increasing horror that this was a deadline that would not be met and that was intended not to be met. The Western Alliance had decided that it needed this war of retribution.

When the war actually began, on the night of 16–17 January 1991, I was in America discussing a screenplay I'd just written about Eastern Europe with the director Bob Rafelson, and I watched the bombs dropping on Baghdad from the comparative safety of a Beverly Hills hotel. I remember the sense of rage and horror and pity in me, feelings that were going to grow and grow over those forty-four horrific days of slaughter. When I got back home, about a week after the outbreak of war, I called Dave Hill and said, 'I think these guys should be building a wall in the Middle East,' and that's really where *The Gulf between Us* started.

I followed the war drowning in rage and pity and an awful sense of impotence, and I began to try and think of how this play might be set in an Iraqi city. As I talk I'm still working on the play – there are sections of it I haven't managed to write yet – and I guess the work will go on up to and beyond the opening night, because that's the ways plays are; I mean you try to get them right on the page before rehearsal, and then in rehearsal you have more writing to do – some that you've done anyway and some that you thought you'd done, but now as you stand it up and work it you see that it needs to be taken further.

How did the theme of the Arabian Nights *occur to you?*

I set myself a kind of literary research task. I wanted to read the Koran, I wanted to read the *Tales of a Thousand and One Nights*, I wanted to read the *Epic of Gilgamesh*, I wanted to read anything and everything that I hadn't read or had forgotten that I'd read, that might help me into the minds of these people at the crossroads of the East and the West. When I began this play all I could think was blood and pain, but the further I got away from the War, the more – I think – balance I got. When I started writing it I discovered that it was going to be a rather strange comedy – and you make these discoveries on the page, you don't make them by agreement with yourself in advance. I also realized that it was not going to be a naturalistic play – that there were going to be elements of it that were shimmering and trembling away from *Tales of a Thousand and One Nights*. What's interesting about the *Thousand and One Nights* is that it's the first literature in Arabic that challenges the rule of the priests and the law-makers and the kings, basing itself in the lives and the language of the people. Then I realized that there was something there that I needed for this play – because this is not a play about presidents and secretary-generals and prime ministers, it's a play about people much closer to the earth – building workers, British building workers and the Arab workers of one kind or another. Also, because the *Thousand and One Nights* was popular it was irreverent, it was satirical, it was comic, and it dealt with the details of everyday life in ways that the Koran or the great epics didn't.

Did you find that when you were writing it, it became a very personal piece, or were you writing it for other people – for all the people who were victims of the Gulf War in one way or another?

I think that writing – all my writing anyway – is probably first of all self-addressed; I mean you write because you can't address the problem without writing: that's the joy and the trap of writing. And there is, I think, in this play a great deal of the pain and the pity and the impotence that I've talked about and that I experienced and continue to experience about these events. But I also know that I want it to be seen in the region, in the Middle East. There was no way that this could be written only for a Western audience. It has to be seen there as well and part of the ambition of The Building Company is to take the play, possibly in this production, out to Palestine and Syria and Iraq if possible.

When I finished the first draft of the play some important things emerged. There is a sense in which the Brits in the play are quite definitely the foreigners – so it's an odd experience reading it and watching it, I suspect, to feel that you're on the outside looking in. Even though the Brits are at the heart of this play, they're not at the moral centre of it. At the moral centre are Arabs who are experiencing this crushing, horrific, punitive, exemplary war which is being handed down to them by the Western Alliance for reasons and values that really don't stand up to even the most cursory scrutiny. To murder a quarter of a million people, at the most conservative estimate, to consign another one or two million people to death in the aftermath and to bomb the country back five thousand years, very nearly, seems to me a pretty unpromising and unpropitious way of trying to create a new world order. Especially when that country was indeed the cradle of civilization and was the origin of so much that we in the West have inherited in the way of art, science, mathematics, medicine, literature, language – even our alphabet.

The country in which the play is set is not named as Iraq. The war is not necessarily that war. It's an un-named country and an un-named city in an un-named war. The references suggest Iraq and the West, but I hope the play generates thoughts and feelings about more than just the most recent conflict. As I said, the moral centre of the play is occupied by Arabs, and because I hadn't known when I began to write that that would be the case, it became very important that this production should honour that event, that discovery. So we decided to cast Arab actors in the four Arab roles, people who had the lived experience of being Arabs and who were, indeed, in the region, living their lives and suffering these traumas, during the Gulf War.

I chose Palestinians partly because the play demands politicized people, people who would, by dint of their own experience, understand the issues that this play deals with. It's not a play

vii

about Palestine or Israel, but Palestinians are much more political than almost anybody else in the region by virtue of their own history; and that hunch, about the essential contribution they would make to the production, has proved right.

I don't know that *The Gulf between Us* is the whole of my reaction to the Gulf War: it's not a documentary, it's not a journalistic piece. It's a kind of dreamplay. My personal reaction will probably come out as poems or song lyrics – I've written some songs already. But the play is certainly emotionally and morally very much about responding to the events of the Gulf War.

Trevor Griffiths, Leeds, 1992

The Gulf between Us was first performed at The West Yorkshire Playhouse, Leeds, on 16 January 1992. The cast was as follows:

O'TOOLE	Dave Hill
RYDER	Paul Slack
CHATTERJEE	Kulvinder Ghir
DR AZIZ	Salwa Nakkarah
ISMAEL	Akram Telawe
ANCIENTS	Yacoub Abu Arafeh
	Ahmad Abo Sal'oum

Director	Trevor Griffiths
Designer	Hayden Griffin
Lighting	Rory Dempster
Associate Director	John Tams
Consultant & Translator	Fateh Azzam
Sound	Mic Pool
Assistant Director	Vicky Featherstone

The play was produced in association with The Building Company.

The author would like to thank Gill Cliff for her help in preparing this text for publication.

ACT ONE

Black.

Slow fade up to chill moonlight over glimpsed desert. Mid-ground, the black outline of a large Bedouin tent.

O'TOOLE *appears foreground in tight golden spot: 'The Gilder's Lamp'. He's large, pushing fifty, with long black hair and a full beard, dressed in the grubby garb of an Arab worker. He carries a large battered grip, an instrument case slung from a shoulder.*

He turns to face the auditorium.

O'TOOLE: 'In the name of Allah
    The Compassionate
    The Merciful
    Blessings and peace eternal
    Upon the Prince of Apostles,
    The Master Muhammad.

'The annals of former generations
Are lessons to the living; men and women
May look back upon the fortunes
Of predecessors and be warned;
And by contemplating
The history of past ages
Be purged of folly.

'Glory to the One who has made
The heritage of antiquity
A guide for our own time . . .'

' . . . For it is from
This heritage are drawn
The Tales of the Arabian Nights
And all that is in them
Of fable and adventure.'
(*He turns to look behind him again.*)

I

Allahu Akbar.
God is good.
(*The spot fades,* O'TOOLE *with it.*
Bleed in –
A coil of Arab voices in quotidian discourse: souk, bazaar,
schoolroom, state radio, tea-shop, mosque. Threads of English
start up, within the coil: an endless lexicon of words invisibly
ingested from the Arabic; a discontinuous mesh of readings
detailing the Near East origins of our alphabet; commercial
jingles; a moral litany from First World leaders justifying the
punitive use of force against Third World intransigents.
The light has gradually thickened to pre-dawn. The voice-coil
eventually gives way to a muezzin calling the faithful to first
prayer. The call holds, grave and pure, for some moments;
becomes, almost seamlessly, a city siren wailing the raid to come.
The siren builds, grows harsh, violent; cuts abruptly as the raid
begins.
In the deep silence, mute cockpit-videos of famous strikes on
bridges, buildings, installations replace the pre-dawn light on the
sky-cyc.
A final Western voice defending the action, then sound and image
fade.
An abrupt plunge into daylight, harsh, strange.
Mid-ground, left, an Arab Ancient spades a slow ant-like path
across a wilderness of rubbled buildings, searching for personal
effects and valuables, a large black bin-liner tied to his waist.
Mid-ground, right, a tent-like structure, green, solitary,
unfathomable, rears above the wasteland.
Foreground, a second Ancient laboriously strings red tape across
an arc of metal stakes driven into the earth.
ISMAEL, *late teens, in shirt, slacks and good shoes, stands*
motionless between mid- and foreground, a kid's football
balanced on his raised right foot.
Silence.
The youth calls out to the two Ancients, holds up his arms, like a
footballer demanding acclaim from the terraces. The Ancients
stop their work to gaze at him; exchange a look; return
impassively to their work.

2

A phone rings. Ismael crosses to an old oil-drum where he's laid his gear, fishes out a phone. The ball goes with him, wobbling at his ankle, the elastic band holding it now clearly visible.)

ISMAEL: *(In Arabic; phone)* Ismael. Yes, sir, it's done, Major, completely screened, the area cordoned off, I'm still waiting for labour . . .

(He listens for some time. Turns upstage to stare at the tent, shakes his head, gradually oppressed by the growing gravity of what he's hearing. Turns downstage again, face grim, concentrated. Frowns. Asks for something to be clarified. Dumbly nods assent.

The call ends. He stows the phone. Stands a moment, as if in shock. Calls the Ancients to leave the site. Stoops to detach the ball. Straps on shoulder holster, slips on his warm-up jacket, pitcher's hat and shades.

Two armed People's Militia arrive, pushing a middle-aged man in bus-driver's uniform ahead of them. The man weeps, distressed, terrified. One of the militiamen hands ISMAEL *a document,* ISMAEL *orders them to take the driver to the tent. The man's pushed roughly to his knees, wails, hopeless.* ISMAEL *reads out the document aloud over the weeping driver, folds it, pockets it, walks behind the man, draws his pistol, lays it to the man's head, fires.*

The driver flops forward in a spray of blood. The militiamen move impassively in to drag him off face down across the rubble. Silence.

ISMAEL *stands, blank, white-faced, swaying and kecking a little. Gathers at the sound of women's voices, raised, anxious, some way down the block. Holsters the pistol. Picks up the phone. Pads out a number. Sees blood on his shoe.)*
Aiee!

O'TOOLE: *(Tape relay)* Wherein it came to pass, on the twenty-first night was told the Tale of the Builder, the Gilder, the Minder and the Gulf between them . . .

(Lights up, less bright.

BILLY RYDER *stands amid the rubble, just arrived, two large grips and a suit-bag in his hands, taking in the Ancients slowly laying a duckboard roadway across the wasteland.*

3

He stacks his gear carefully, rubs his eyes, whacked; sniffs, sniffs again.)

RYDER: (*Calling the Ancients*) This it?

(They look at him.)

This the er . . .?

(Nothing.) OK, forget it . . .

(He wanders over to the tent, deliberates a moment, moves towards the flap-entrance, freezes as a volley of shots, off, scatters the shrieking women.

ISMAEL *in fast, bawling back a question at a perimeter guard. The guard responds: the women have retreated.* ISMAEL *checks watch and sun, chivvies the Ancients, who work on as before, mute, lava-like; flicks the kid's ball up into the air, punts it in the direction of the tent; sees* RYDER.)

ISMAEL: Hey. You.

RYDER: Talkin' to me?

ISMAEL: Over here.

(ISMAEL sits on his oil-drum, studies a clipboard of papers. RYDER collects his gear, approaches, some tension evident inside the self-assurance.)

Name?

RYDER: Ryder. Billy.

ISMAEL: I.D. (*Takes it.*) Ryder William. What's Billy?

RYDER: It's short for William.

ISMAEL: Mm. You here alone?

RYDER: Ahunh. Listen, son . . .

ISMAEL: I'm promised two persons . . .

RYDER: (*Looking round*) Aye, well, you're one short. (*Takes I.D. back.*) Do me a favour, will you, call the head honcho, I've got a letter from Colonel Faqir down at the Water Filtration Plant . . .

ISMAEL: What is it concerning? This letter?

RYDER: Well, it's actually addressed to the senior man here . . .

ISMAEL: Nevertheless . . .

RYDER: OK. Number one, I've been slavin' down at the water plant since the dawn raid, OK?, an' I'm knackered. Number two, I'm meant to be getting an exit visa an' a ticket out today, I mean the Ministry gave me their word, anyway

4

they're not at the hotel, so I need a couple of hours to call in
at the office and erm . . . collect 'em. You understand any o'
this?

(ISMAEL *stands, checks his watch, looks at the sky.*)

ISMAEL: OK, Ryder Billy, I show you the job . . .

RYDER: Excuse me, you don't seem to be hearing me, hey . . .

ISMAEL: (*Hard*) Hey!

RYDER: (*Fast*) What?

ISMAEL: Don't hey to me. I do heying.

RYDER: That's fine.

ISMAEL: You bet.

RYDER: (*Letter in hands; reasonable*) I just wanted to draw your
attention to the fact that this is an official correspondence, I
mean someone in authority ought to read it . . .
(*Silence.*)

ISMAEL: OK. I see to it.

(*He puts his hand out.* RYDER *looks at it.*)

RYDER: How do you mean?

ISMAEL: (*Telephone*) I read it to my Major.

RYDER: Oh. Right. Excellent. (*Hands it over. Looks around him.*)
You got labour?

(ISMAEL *indicates the two Ancients.*)

Terrific. I meant craftsmen, you know, brickies . . . Splat
clunk.

ISMAEL: A person's coming . . .

RYDER: I hope so, cos my job's not hands-on, I'm more
management . . .

ISMAEL: (*Sharp*) Hey.

RYDER: What?

ISMAEL: I'm the boss.

RYDER: Sure.

ISMAEL: And.

RYDER: Yes?

ISMAEL: I have a boss.

RYDER: I understand.

ISMAEL: So. This building here inside . . . a missile came through
a window and out the back wall. My boss instructs Ismael
mend the wall before sundown, no if no but, before dark

5

(*Looks at sky*) you see the picture . . .? I show you the job.

RYDER: Ah, I see, it's a complete misunderstanding, time's of the essence, we're saying the same thing . . . I was just about to suggest I size the job up, work out what you need, how long it'll tek, while you can be reading the Colonel's letter to your Major . . . Division of labour.

(*Silence. The men eye each other; a slightly scary stand-off.*)

(*Tacking into sincerity*) Look, er . . . Ismael, that's your name, right? D'you mind . . .? Ismael, you have every right to be angry at what the white . . . at what the West is doing to your people and your country . . . It is, it's horrible, horrible, but . . . I could've left with everyone else, spent Christmas with the wife and kiddie, I chose to stay, I chose to help, right up to the deadline and beyond, right up to this day, I put my life on the line, told the Ministry my services were at their disposal, you know . . . Then three weeks ago I got news my wife had been very seriously injured in a car crash, a bus . . . they say the driver was drunk, I don't know . . . (*Sniffing, reeling him in*) I am not trying to be obstructive, friend, I'm just fairly desperate to get home, you know . . .? (*Looks at his watch.*) What can I say . . .?

(*Silence again.* ISMAEL *checks the sky.*)

ISMAEL: You got tough shit, Ryder Billy. (*A new commotion erupts down at the tent-side perimeter line, men's voices lifting in fervid anger.*)

You size the job. I call the Major.

RYDER: (*Hand out*) God bless you.

(ISMAEL *takes it.*)

It's a deal.

ISMAEL: You have my hand, you have my word.

RYDER: You're a brick, sir.

(*A call from a militiaman labouring up from tent-side perimeter.* ISMAEL *takes him in. Watches* RYDER *readying for work.*)

ISMAEL: Hey.

RYDER: Yessir . . .

ISMAEL: In here is. Ancient holy place. You stay out of. Such a place is not for your eyes. (*In Arabic*) Yes, I'm coming.

(*The approaching militiaman stops on the crest of the mounded rubble. A second man lumbers up behind him.*)

You understand?

RYDER: Absolutely.

(ISMAEL *crosses to speak with the guards. He gives one of them
Ryder's letter and murmured instructions, sends him on his way.*
RYDER, *out of sight now in the lee of the tent, peels seamlessly from
his studied zeal, chuckling as he lights a fag and begins changing
into working gear.*)

Dear dear dear. Like takin' sweets off a child. Bloody wife in a
car crash, Jesus, there's one born every day . . . Perfect. Just
what I've bin lookin' for . . .

ISMAEL: (*Calling*) Hey.

RYDER: (*Fast*) Yessir.

ISMAEL: (*Phone up*) I see where second man is, OK?

RYDER: Fine. No time to waste.

(*More din from the tent-side perimeter.* ISMAEL *completes the call,
instructs the remaining militiaman to guard the site, yells at the
Ancients to help* RYDER, *hurries off to deal with the disturbance.
The Ancients plod across to the tent, begin peeling away the
entrance flaps.* RYDER *weighs up what's on site, lays out tools and
a metre-stick, closes in to assess the damage.
Little by little, the rear wall of a pre-Muslim shrine is uncovered, a
huge chunk of masonry bitten out by the hit, the surviving
stonework charred by flash-marks. Beyond the hole, a second
hanging thick-mesh screen blocking further access; through which,
suggested rather than seen, a solitary stained-glass window tinily
lights the blackness.*
RYDER *feeds readings and measurements into his Psion II. The
Ancients gaze at him incuriously.*)

(*Uncomfortable*) OK. Piss off. Scram.

(*They stand; mute, immovable.*)

Go on, get outa here . . . Imshi, Imshi.

(*He claps his hands behind them, like a man shooing geese. The
Ancients seep back to their duckboards.* RYDER *busies himself
measuring and feeding in, launched on a tuneless version of 'Let
Me Go'; turns for a moment to check the sky, as a distant siren
starts up to the west; sniffs, keys his Psion for print-out, reads
it.*)

This'll be no pushover either . . .

(O'TOOLE *emerges from the shrine. He's in frayed denim shorts, an old Man United shirt and sandals, carries his Arab work gear on one arm. Stretches. Yawns.*)

(*Seriously startled*) Jesus Christ, who the fuck're you . . .?

(O'TOOLE *checks watch, sky; listens a moment, as the aerial attack begins some miles away.*)

O'TOOLE: (*Strong East Lancs voice*) You woke me up with your yammering. I was taking a nap.

RYDER: Unbelievable. Ha. I thought I were t'last on board, put it there, old son, Billy Ry–

O'TOOLE: (*Uninterested*) Ryder, yeah. Heard you hustling the kid.

(*He re-enters the tent, reaches out his gear from beyond the thick mesh, carries it out on to the site. Checks his feet; the shoes are caked in a black, shiny goo.*)

RYDER: (*Tracking him*) In there? 'S off limits, din't anyone tell you, you'll get me shot . . .

O'TOOLE: (*Thinks; frowns*) Why would they shoot *you*?

RYDER: (*Back foot*) Because I'm bloody meant to be in charge . . .

O'TOOLE: Are you? (*Shakes head.*) You could be in for a really trying day, sunshine.

RYDER: What, that? (*The hole*) Coupla hours, piecea cake, two brickies on the job . . .

O'TOOLE: You're a brickie, are you?

RYDER: 'S matter of fact, I run my own firm, but yes, that's my trade . . .

O'TOOLE: (*Looking around*) Where's the other one?

RYDER: What?

O'TOOLE: You said two.

RYDER: Well, what're you?

O'TOOLE: Not a brickie, son, that much I can tell you . . .

(*He sits. Fiddles in his instrument case, brings out a can of Stone's. Looks at feet again.*)

RYDER: Oh, Christ. (*Studies him.*) Have I missed something . . .? I mean, who are you? How come you're here in the first place?

O'TOOLE: No comment.

8

RYDER: 'S that mean?

O'TOOLE: Whatever you want it to.

RYDER: You're trouble. I can smell it.

O'TOOLE: (*Studying sandals*) 'S probably these. Trod in something back there. Cat-shit mebbe.
(*He begins trying to clean them, smells the stuff, stares back at the hole, looks again at* RYDER.)
I can get you a brickie.

RYDER: Oh aye? What you gonna do, ring the job shop?

O'TOOLE: Please yourself.

RYDER: I can lay the buggers meself if I have to, there's time . . .

O'TOOLE: (*Checking sky; listening*) Don't count on it.
(*He wets a finger, holds it up for the wind.*)

RYDER: How d'you mean?

O'TOOLE: That's the refineries being blitzed again. Wind picks up, you're gonna be needing braille.
(RYDER *listens. Bites his lip. Looks at* O'TOOLE.)

RYDER: Who are you?

O'TOOLE: Name's O'Toole.

RYDER: What are you doin' here?

O'TOOLE: 'S a long story. Yours too, eh?
(*He grins, hands* RYDER *the can. Begins slipping into his Arab work trousers. Calls something in Arabic to the guard above; the guy tells him to wait.*)

RYDER: You're a weird fucker, I'll tell you.
(O'TOOLE *gives a scary chuckle.*)
How come you can get a brickie?

O'TOOLE: I know the turf, friend. 'S my patch.
(*A woman calls, another answers, another; regrouping. The guard picks up his rifle, dumps his fag.* ISMAEL's *voice calling, still distant, on the approach.*)

RYDER: Fuck me. Teks all sorts . . .

O'TOOLE: (*Quiet*) Put it this way. I'm all you've got.

RYDER: Oh aye? I've got a deal with the kid. He does his stuff, I'm out of here.

O'TOOLE: Sure. 'You got tough shit, Ryder Billy.' Do me a favour.

RYDER: I'm telling you, that letter's for real, two hundred quidsworth of it.

9

(O'TOOLE *chuckles again. Picks up the ball, twirls it on his finger.
The guard calls something down to the approaching* ISMAEL.)

O'TOOLE: You haven't the first idea, have you? You've got Shias
ready to riot over there, you've got women going crazy the
other side, I haven't worked out what the hell's going on here,
but I'd lay a small wager it's gonna be something truly awful, I
mean a lot worse than Blackpool, a lot worse, and you think
you've got something going with the *kid*? (*His eyes burn black
across the space between them.*) Trust me. Not a request. You
muck around with Ismael, you'll get us *all* shot . . .

(ISMAEL *crests the rubble ridge, exchanges words with the guard,
begins the descent to join them.*)

(*To be heard, a seamless segue*) . . . The guy says, 'This doesn't
seem so bad, knee-deep in dog-shit, sure, but I always
imagined Hell'd be a lot worse than this,' then the door opens,
this bugger with horns and a tail blows his whistle and shouts,
'Tea break over, back on your heads . . .'

ISMAEL: (*Beckoning*) Hey, you. You're late. Where you been?

(*A moment, as* O'TOOLE *studies the youth.*)

O'TOOLE: Graveyard. Burying the dead.

ISMAEL: I.D. (*Takes it. Checks clipboard.*) How you say this?

O'TOOLE: O'Toole.

(ISMAEL *hands it back, studies him carefully.*)

ISMAEL: O'Toole.

(*The distant explosions tail off. The two stand in silence, locked. A
siren sounds all-clear. Silence.*)

OK. (*To* RYDER) You size what we need, mister?

RYDER: (*Print-out in hand*) 'S all here.

ISMAEL: No problem, hunh?

(RYDER *glances at* O'TOOLE, *who's studying the sky.*)

RYDER: Be a push. It can be done.

ISMAEL: You say the boys what you need, they fetch and carry,
truck's on the corner here . . . (*Yells instructions in Arabic at the
Ancients*) Let's go, let's go. (*To* O'TOOLE; *sharp*) You stay
here.

RYDER: I was wondering if there was any word on the visa
thing . . .

(*Silence.*)

ISMAEL: My Major speak with the Ministry, they check. They give him a strong maybe.

RYDER: Strong maybe, hunh? (*Another glance at* O'TOOLE.) Fine. Fine.
(*He leaves with the Ancients.* ISMAEL *watches a moment, slips off his jacket, casually repositions his pistol, sits down for a smoke, his hands trembling a touch.* O'TOOLE *collects a long-handled shovel, begins clearing a work area around the shrine wall.* ISMAEL *watches, broods. Takes out phone, keys a number, rattles something in Arabic, we hear* 'O'TOOLE' *twice. Pockets phone.*)

ISMAEL: Your team, yes?

O'TOOLE: What?

ISMAEL: Your team. Man United.

O'TOOLE: Right.

ISMAEL: Good team, eh?

O'TOOLE: The best.

ISMAEL: Red devils.

O'TOOLE: Right.

ISMAEL: Sir Matt Bussaby.

O'TOOLE: Yeah.

ISMAEL: You skinhead, hunh?
(O'TOOLE *smiles.*)
You know Gazza?

O'TOOLE: Gaza? Never bin, no.

ISMAEL: Gazza. Gazza?

O'TOOLE: Gazza, right. Sure.

ISMAEL: Great, hunh?

O'TOOLE: Pretty good. Bit of a prick.

ISMAEL: Bit of a prick, sure. You wanna sell?

O'TOOLE: What?

ISMAEL: Ten dinar. I give you.

O'TOOLE: Uhunh.

ISMAEL: Fifteen.

O'TOOLE: You like it?

ISMAEL: 'S OK.

O'TOOLE: Cost me two hundred.
(ISMAEL *thinks.*)

ISMAEL: OK, twenty.
(O'TOOLE *laughs*.)
What?
O'TOOLE: Tell you what. Maybe I'll give it you. How's that
sound?
ISMAEL: Why?
O'TOOLE: Because.
ISMAEL: Because.
O'TOOLE: We'll see.
(*Phone again.* ISMAEL *answers: gets the result of the check on*
O'TOOLE; *is told to expect* DR AZIZ, *from the Ministry, on site to
help with the women.* O'TOOLE *works on, always within
earshot.*
*The Ancients have reappeared, struggling an antique diesel-
powered cement-mixer on to the site.* BILLY RYDER *follows,
carrying tools and gear.*)
RYDER: I'm gonna need help, chief, these boys don't understand
a word I say . . .
ISMAEL: I fix.
(*He hurls instructions to the guard above, who bawls down to the
perimeter for assistance; snarls abuse at the Ancients; generally
puts himself about.*)
Let's go, let's go . . .
RYDER: Get these sorted, will you? I'll start getting the blocks
in . . .
(O'TOOLE *pitches in. Two militiamen arrive;* ISMAEL *directs
them to the truck.*)
(*Sotto*) 'S happenin'?
O'TOOLE: This guy's in trouble.
RYDER: How? Shit. What d'you mean?
ISMAEL: (*Loud*) 'S go!
(RYDER *and the helpers move back off to the truck.* O'TOOLE
begins stripping off the shirt.)
Where I saw you?
O'TOOLE: Spent a lot of time here. I was in this place before you
were born, son.
ISMAEL: O'Toole.
O'TOOLE: O'Toole. Here.

(*He wraps the shirt into a ball, underarms it across the site into* ISMAEL's *waiting arms.*)
All yours. You're on the team.
ISMAEL: (*Slowly*) Why you do this?
O'TOOLE: I'm fifty next month. It's starting to look foolish.
(*The youth deliberates the binding gift; eventually stoops to stow it in his case; lifts his head to listen as a fierce high-pitch ululation sets up around the women's perimeter.* O'TOOLE *pads across to look and listen. Fear and grief wash the site.*)
What is that?
(ISMAEL *gives a fierce look, returns to packing the shirt.*)
ISMAEL: Just women. It's nothing.
O'TOOLE: Friend, if you have a problem . . .
ISMAEL: (*Standing*) Problem? I have no problem.
O'TOOLE: A man without problems has a problem.
ISMAEL: (*Staring off; the howling thickening*) I follow orders, no problem.
(*He looks up suddenly, stares at the sky.*
The light begins to bleed away, strengthens for a moment, darkens again, as a pall of smoke blocks the sun – continues to end of the act.
The returning helpers stop, heads lifted, to look.
ISMAEL *barks at them to move. A guard hurries up from the women's perimeter, reports the situation.* ISMAEL *sends him back, prepares to follow, stops on the rubble ridge, turns to scan the labouring traffic.* RYDER's *back, bossing the boys, organizing materials in the rough work area.*)
No if no but, Ryder Billy. Tick tick, eh? You play the game, Ismael will do you OK. (*Looks at* O'TOOLE.) You fuck him around, he blows your legs off. Tick tick.
(*He calls an instruction to the remaining guard, moves off.*)
RYDER: (*For* ISMAEL; *keen to please*) Come on, let's get crackin', lads, we haven't got all bloody day . . . Watch that, for Christ's sake, no no no, like this, see, carry it like this . . .
(*Breezeblocks, tools, lime, sand, cement, water and a rough do-it-yourself scaffolding gradually find their way from truck to work area.* RYDER *nips and harries throughout, nervily checking the minder's whereabouts.*

O'TOOLE *gathers his Arab work tunic, slips it on, carries his bag and instrument case to safer ground downstage. Opens another can of Stone's. Stares out at the city below.*

RYDER *sees him, checks Ismael's gone, joins him.*)

RYDER: You're not getting ready t'do a bunk, are you?

(O'TOOLE *looks at him calmly, looks back at the city.*)

Why you wearing that stuff?

O'TOOLE: Why are they?

RYDER: Cos they're fucking Arabs, I don't know.

O'TOOLE: Deep. You've really given that some thought.

RYDER: Listen, don't piss around, we've gotta pull together on this one. You said the kid was in trouble, what's he told you?

O'TOOLE: The kid's scared. He's on the line with this thing, you can smell it . . .

RYDER: Who gives a shit? Trouble for these buggers is leverage for me, man, that's all I care about. I've shelled out a small fortune down at that bleedin' office 'n' I'm getting nowhere, they're just milking me dry . . . I've had three weeks o' this nightmare, I've gotta get out, I can't take this, I made a deal, they're fucking me over. You put your back into this one for me and I'll see you right and that's a promise. Now just tell me what you can do and I'll work round you, OK . . . I mean you do have a trade, right, just . . . I mean what are you?

(*The howling breaks down.* ISMAEL's *voice, megaphoned, addressing the women.* O'TOOLE *listens.*)

O'TOOLE: (*Eventually*) All right. I'm not sure if you're ready for this, Ryder Billy . . .

RYDER: (*Nervy*) What?

O'TOOLE: I'm a reporter. For the *Sun*. Undercover.

(*Silence.*)

RYDER: Oh Jesus.

O'TOOLE: (*Deliberate*) No no. You're supposed to say, 'Don't be daft, the *Sun* doesn't have reporters . . .'

(*He chuckles, oddly pleased.*)

RYDER: Funny. Ha bloody ha. I think the sun's shrivelled your brain-pan or someat. Personally, I don't get the joke . . .

O'TOOLE: Look at it (*the site, the world*). Look at it, will you. The new world order. We're the joke.

14

(RYDER *surveys the scene. The Ancients have squatted in the* *sand to rest.*)

RYDER: (*Calling*) Hey, come on, let's be having you, there's plenty more where that came from . . .
(*He gives* O'TOOLE *a final wither, returns to his tasks, eventually leads the Ancients to the cement-mixer. His efforts to start it up and make mortar cover most of the next sequence.*
O'TOOLE *opens his instrument case, takes out a dulcimer, squats cross-legged, lays it on his lap.*
A golden spot grows around him, as the lowering light behind dims the work action to a sort of lurid shadowplay.
O'TOOLE *tunes briefly, plays. The sounds are picked up, enlarged, redistributed, remade; voices in Arabic thread in and out; male, female, anger, grief; fade eventually back to* O'TOOLE'*s unaccompanied dulcimer.*)

O'TOOLE: Outside the besieged city, the massed ranks of the Christian host from the north pitilessly prepare the next assault, cold in their resolve to render life impossible for the unfortunate citizenry huddled within and so bring the Caliph to his knees. Already, between one moon and another, their great engines of war, their mangonels and petraries, have turned the days into nightmare, poisoning wells, destroying riverbanks, killing crops and livestock, leaving infants to suckle in vain on shrivelled breasts. Smoke covers the noonday sun like a death-shroud; deadly vapours, cries of the bereft and the dying, choke the narrow streets; sweet order collapses into murky chaos. And down in the Caliph's courtyard, so recently despoiled by enemy fire, our heroes scheme and plot their survival in a tiny war-play of their own. The Builder smells advantage on the poisoned air; the youthful Minder searches for manhood on the sticky paths of duty; and Finbar, our Wandering Gilder, his plans deep laid and all but ready to spring, struggles to recall the details of his tale from the wearying darkness that engulfs him. A phrase bubbles in his brain-pan: 'One clean heart, one clean heart.' What? Who? Ha. Of course. He had quite forgotten. The Good Doctor.
(*He looks up suddenly. A woman appears, front of stage, on the*

*other side of the red-tape picket: Arab dress and headgear, strong
leather briefcase. She takes in the scene for a moment, steps over
the tape, triggering a return to the previous lighting state.*
O'TOOLE *begins returning hammers and instrument to the case.
She calls the militiaman: gives name, position, business, asks for
the man in charge. The guard points to the women's perimeter,
indicates she should await his return.*
*She takes some paces towards the shrine, the guard calls, shakes
his head; she nods, wanders back to front-of-stage, stops to light a
cigarette, gives* O'TOOLE *a perfunctory look, gravely scans the
sorry site again, turns to gaze out at the city.*)

DR AZIZ: (*A murmur; remembering*) 'My name is Ozymandias,
king of kings:

> Look on my works, ye Mighty, and despair!
> Nothing beside remains. Round the decay
> Of that colossal wreck, boundless and bare,
> The lone and level sands stretch far away.'

(*She sniffs.*)

O'TOOLE: Shelley.

(*She turns sharply, as if seeing him for the first time. He smiles,
stands, salutes her with his can of Stone's.*)

DR AZIZ: Are you . . .? What are you?

O'TOOLE: Just part of the circus.

DR AZIZ: But British, yes?

O'TOOLE: (*After thought*) Yes.

DR AZIZ: Strange.

O'TOOLE: Yes. (*Beat.*) I wish there were something to offer you, I
have only this (*shows her the can*) . . . I realize it's not quite
the thing . . .

DR AZIZ: Well, as it happens I'm a Christian, but alcohol doesn't
agree with me, thank you . . .

O'TOOLE: Me too. That's why I stick to this.

(*She smiles. A silence. She turns away, gazes again at the city.*
O'TOOLE *checks the site.* RYDER *gets the diesel mixer to start.
The helpers applaud. It putters on for a few moments, then dies,
the applause with it.* RYDER *curses.*)

I love this city. Do you see the Monument? Bottom of July
26th Boulevard, just before the Southern Highway. Sixty-

five metres high, is that. We finished that the day before the
first bombs fell. See the gold on the President's shoulders?
Mine. If you were closer, much closer, you'd see he has a
gold tooth. I did that too.

DR AZIZ: Does he have a gold tooth?

O'TOOLE: He does now.

(*He smiles, sucks on the can.*)

DR AZIZ: You're a building worker?

O'TOOLE: Ahunh.

DR AZIZ: Who reads poetry.

O'TOOLE: Why not?

(*They exchange a look, return to the city.*)

DR AZIZ: Aren't you afraid?

O'TOOLE: Oh yes.

DR AZIZ: But you stayed on.

O'TOOLE: Yes.

DR AZIZ: Because you love the city?

O'TOOLE: I like to leave places when I'm ready. As it happens,
I've been waiting for someone, a friend. He's been detained.
(*The women begin wailing, drowning out ISMAEL's
mollifications. DR AZIZ turns to listen. Guards bawl for quiet;
the women subside; ISMAEL's voice reasserts, a touch desperate.*)

DR AZIZ: (*Calling the Guard; in Arabic*) Tell him I'm here, will
you, I need to speak with them . . .
(*The guy wavers.*)
Go!
(*He leaves for the women's perimeter. DR AZIZ lights another
cigarette.*)
God help us all.

O'TOOLE: Amen.
(*RYDER shepherds carriers towards the work area, transferring
bags of lime, cement, etc.*)

RYDER: (*Calling*) Come on, O'Toole, let's go, let's go . . .
(*O'TOOLE waves, fastens his instrument case, drains his can.*)

O'TOOLE: Nice to meet you, ma'am.

DR AZIZ: Indeed.

O'TOOLE: What will you tell them? The women?

DR AZIZ: I'll tell them the truth. The children are perfectly safe,

17

a bus took them to the Al-Mansur shelter across the river last evening, we'll keep them there until it's safe to return them . . .

O'TOOLE: God's wounds. I see. One of these was a school . . .

DR AZIZ: A crèche. I'm crèche supervisor for the Sector . . .

O'TOOLE: The kids didn't come home after the raid . . .

DR AZIZ: It's our policy to bus them to safety, this the mothers know, but their fears are understandable . . . I heard the crèche was hit before I heard they were in the shelter. It was not easy . . .

(*Silence.* ISMAEL's *voice, on the approach, hoarse from his efforts.*)

RYDER: (*Calling*) For Christ's sake, will you get over here, man . . .

(O'TOOLE *ignores him, focus utterly on the woman.*)

DR AZIZ: As to how your countrymen can justify a district crèche and a dozen dwellings in a workers' suburb as legitimate targets . . .

(*She turns to look at him.*)

RYDER: (*Calling*) You're gonna get me shot, O'Toole, you know that, don't you . . .

O'TOOLE: (*Still*) Try to think of it as 'collateral damage', ma'am. Seems to do the trick on my side of the water.

(*She looks at him fiercely, the irony having trouble registering.* ISMAEL *arrives, the militiaman in tow, scrambles down the slope towards* DR AZIZ, *draws her to one side to fill her in and set her to work on the women.*

O'TOOLE *joins* RYDER *in the work area. Light slowly builds again, as smoke clears the sun. The Ancients stand by as if elsewhere. The helpers have returned to perimeter duties.*)

RYDER: (*Looking up from his mortar-mixing*) Wind's changin'. We'll have two hours at least, I lay, you labour, a doddle . . .

O'TOOLE: (*Checking sky*) You're gonna need another brickie, boy. Tek my word.

RYDER: Give it a rest, will you. I've got this licked. (*Checking the talking couple*) What's the bird here for?

O'TOOLE: One o' these was a nursery.

RYDER: Oh shit.

O'TOOLE: Save the tears, the babs were elsewhere.

>   (*Ululations set up again.* ISMAEL *grows aggressive,* DR AZIZ
>   *reluctantly accepts his argument.*)
>   They're scared the women'll overrun the site 'n' stop the
>   work. She's sent to calm 'em.
>   (ISMAEL *calls the guard to show* DR AZIZ *down to the women's
>   perimeter. Phones his Major. Reports.*)

RYDER: (*Back to his mixing*) A nursery. What a carry-on.

O'TOOLE: 'S wrong with the mixer?

RYDER: They're out of oil, aren't they. Couldn't organize a shag
>   in a brothel . . .

O'TOOLE: So. Are you gonna back me up or what?

RYDER: What you talkin' about?

O'TOOLE: I'm gonna tell the kid we need another trowel . . .

RYDER: (*Blowing, fierce*) No fuckin' way, José, forget it, this is
>   my job, my deal, I'm fast, man, never mind the quality,
>   check the speed, you start buggerin' around there's no tellin'
>   what'll happen . . . (*He gathers himself*) I'm gonna show you
>   what to do, OK?

O'TOOLE: (*Calm*) You won't be told, will you.

RYDER: Just. Let it lie.

>   (*A glance at Ismael, ending phone call.*) You put your back
>   into this, I'll get you out of here, that's a promise.

ISMAEL: (*Call over; calling*) Hey! Ryder Billy!

>   (RYDER *turns abruptly.* ISMAEL *holds an envelope aloft in his
>   hand. Beckons him over with it.*)

RYDER: Yessir. (*To* O'TOOLE) This is gonna work. I know it is.

>   (O'TOOLE *collects a sledgehammer, steps inside the hole, begins
>   flattening out irregularities in the fringing masonry.* RYDER
>   *clambers across to join* ISMAEL. *The women quieten;* DR AZIZ's
>   *megaphone voice lifts, strong and clear, in the silence, inviting
>   them to take tea with her in a neighbourhood school canteen.
>   Murmurs of assent. Voices fade.*)

ISMAEL: Passport.

RYDER: Passport? 'S in my bag.

ISMAEL: Fetch.

>   (RYDER *twitches back to fetch his passport.* O'TOOLE *chuckles
>   softly as he nears him.*)

RYDER: (*Returning*) Look, I'm not sure what this is about, friend, where I come from this here is a pretty sacred document . . .

(ISMAEL *checks it, tucks it in his pocket.*)

Hey, come on . . .

ISMAEL: Hey. I hey. OK? (*Hands him the envelope.*) Visa, ticket. You build the wall. I give you passport. You bugger off.

RYDER: (*Thumbing contents*) Jesus. You came through, Ismael.

ISMAEL: My word, my hand.

RYDER: You scratch my back, eh?

(*Silence.*)

ISMAEL: (*Frowning*) We ready?

RYDER: Sure thing.

ISMAEL: (*A question there*) This O'Toole.

RYDER: Comedian.

ISMAEL: Funny man. Jokha.

RYDER: I can handle him.

ISMAEL: He help, hunh? He can do splat clunk fast?

RYDER: He'll do what he's told.

(ISMAEL's *head flicks away towards the men's perimeter. Distant approaching sounds of men's voices on the march. Guards call nervously to each other.*)

ISMAEL: You build the wall, you perform great service, Ryder Billy. That's a message from my Major. In daylight we can keep away these madmen, these looters and criminals. Come the night, come the bombs, set your clock by it, how we do it then, eh? Many holy things, hunh?

RYDER: Got it.

ISMAEL: Here.

(*He holds out the passport.* RYDER *takes it.*)

(*Soft*) Let's go.

(*He clambers off to speak with the guard.* RYDER *returns to the shrine, gets busy gathering tools, looks around for* O'TOOLE.)

RYDER: (*Sotto*) Hey. You there? For Christ's sake, O'Toole, give me a break, will you . . . (*Approaches hole; nervous*) You in there? (*Peers in.*) Listen, I've got mine, I can get yours, trust me . . .

(O'TOOLE's *head and shoulders slowly emerge at roof height from*

20

beneath the covering canvas. His face is still, expressionless,
fixed on nothing.)
(*Edging nervously across the wall*) He's fucked off, I know it
. . . Bastard. Selfish old get. Shit! Serve him right if they
bloody shoot him . . .
(O'TOOLE *directs his gaze down on the twitching* RYDER, *who*
chunners on, panic rising.)
(*Out again; hoarse, urgent*) Are you there? Where are you?

O'TOOLE: (*Soft*) Up here.

RYDER: (*Too loud*) Aagh!

O'TOOLE: Sh. You'll wake the dead.

RYDER: What's that?
(*He indicates the length of scorched coaxial cable in* O'TOOLE'*s*
hand. O'TOOLE *looks at it; shrugs.*)
What're you doi–?

O'TOOLE: Just checkin'. No point buildin' a wall if the roof's
gone . . .

RYDER: Is it?

O'TOOLE: Roof's fine. Burnt to buggery but it'll do.
(*He swings down in a sort of forward roll, using the lintel as a*
bar. Lands with a grin at RYDER'*s feet.*)
So. Are you winnin', Ryder Billy?
(RYDER *takes out the envelope, holds it up.*)

RYDER: I'm doin' OK.

O'TOOLE: (*Eyeing it*) Tell me.

RYDER: Visa. Ticket to ride.

O'TOOLE: Nice work. All you need now is your passport
back . . .
(*The march has reached the perimeter. Cries, chants, slogans, a*
few shots loosed into the air, the sudden pop and whoosh of
petrol bombs, frenzy building. ISMAEL *crosses the ridge at*
speed, calls down to the other guard post, militiamen hurry
across to reinforce the men's perimeter. ISMAEL *calls his Major.*
O'TOOLE *watches it all with care.* RYDER *produces his*
passport, draws O'TOOLE'*s focus back with it.*)
I don't believe it.

RYDER: O ye of little faith.

O'TOOLE: You checked it? The visa?

21

RYDER: Course I checked it.

O'TOOLE: You read the language, d'ye?

RYDER: What?

(O'TOOLE *holds his hand out*, RYDER *bites his lip, hands him the envelope.* O'TOOLE *studies the contents.*

Warfare erupts, down at the men's perimeter. Volleys ring out, screams and moans of men hit on the scatter, several petrol bombs reach in to the site, gutter out in sand and rubble. ISMAEL *stands immobile on the ridge, staring off, hand on gun butt inside jacket: little Napoleon.*

O'TOOLE *looks up from the visa and ticket, stares in silence at* RYDER. *Shakes his head.*)

What?

O'TOOLE: (*Slow*) Bad news, boy.

RYDER: What?

O'TOOLE: Looks like you pulled it off.

RYDER: (*Snatching it back*) Give it 'ere. Prick. How can it be bad news . . .?

O'TOOLE: We'll find out.

RYDER: You were wrong, just admit it. This may be your patch, O'Toole, I know the score, OK?

O'TOOLE: You may be right.

RYDER: I didn't get where I am today by being wrong, believe you me.

(O'TOOLE *scans the appalling wasteland: no comment. Offstage, the engagement stutters on. Men moan.*)

O'TOOLE: Billy. You're OK. I like you. I like your spirit. I like your optimism. It's rare. I was wrong. You're smart. You conned the shit outa the little sod. Comprehensively. Rafael O'Toole. Put it there.

(RYDER *takes the large mitt.*)

I think we can do business.'

RYDER: *First* we can do some work, OK?

O'TOOLE: Putty in your hands, Mr Ryder.

(*They share a chuckle, move into work mode.*

Music, patched-in words, on relay.

Elements of their talk lift and fall back, as they work. The engagement, off, has ended; its sounds abate. The Ancients

22

*struggle on another load of blocks, begin their precarious trek across
the site.*

*ISMAEL leaves his watch, sits halfway down the rubble slope to
monitor the Brits' progress. Smokes. Lies on his back to stare at the
sky. Eventually takes out his phone, keys a number, asks for
someone, waits, gets through. His talk, in Arabic, eventually
readable as being with his girlfriend, patches into theirs.)*

RYDER: Keep these (*blocks*) about this high, will you.

O'TOOLE: Right you are, chief.

RYDER: Here, take this. (*Hands him string.*) Keep us straight.
Secrets of the craft. You'll get the hang of it.

*(ISMAEL's chat is light, bantering, shy, hesitant, vulnerable: for
these minutes, the war has no presence for either of them. He has
asked her to marry him; wants her answer.*

*RYDER lays the first blocks, establishing rhythm and work pattern.
O'TOOLE becomes part of it, replacing each block taken from the
block stack with a new one. Each time RYDER comes back up for
one he calls out its number, a deep work habit, part of his process.)*
What's the story anyway?

O'TOOLE: Been waiting for a guy, we've got a job in Java waiting on
us, little devil's been held up . . .
(RYDER chuckles, shakes his head.)
How 'bout you, Bill?

RYDER: Long story. Deals 'n' stuff. Bit above the Paddy's head I
think, O'Toole.

O'TOOLE: Try me.
(On the phone, ISMAEL's talk becomes serious, even painful.)

RYDER: I'm standin' there, British Airways, queuin' a buy a ticket
out, hundreds of us down there, scramblin' a get 'ome . . .
terrific din . . .
(Long silence. He's back there, in the moment.) An' like
everything went quiet, like that . . . An' I had this brilliant
thought: what if there's no war? Four weeks on and this
place'll be doin' business as usual. And he who dares, wins.
Next day I'm down the Ministry doin' deals, talk about a field
of clover, there's queues formin' round me, The Brit who
refused to Quit. I've contracts for *millions* in that bag there . . .
(They work on in silence, rhythm, pattern, calls returning.

ISMAEL's *tone is now angry, jealous, persistent; a boy.*
RYDER *begins laying the second course.*)

O'TOOLE: (*Eventually*) Pity about the war.

(RYDER *snaps a look at him.* O'TOOLE's *deep in work, as if unawares.*)

RYDER: (*Suspicions abating*) Deep. You really gave that some thought.

(*He chuckles, swells, pleased with himself.* O'TOOLE *smiles. Each dips again to his work.* O'TOOLE's *up at once.*)

O'TOOLE: So when d'you reckon I should be hittin' the kid with *my* list, William?

RYDER: I'm workin' on it, OK? What fuckin' *list*?

O'TOOLE: 'S not a list, just a coupla things . . .

(RYDER *swings up for a block, numbers it out loud, glares up at* O'TOOLE. ISMAEL *giggles at something she's told him.*)

RYDER: Visa. Ticket to ride. List ends. If I can. That's the deal. (*They work on.*)

Don't get greedy, kid's on a tightrope, imagine what he's going to be like when we get up to here (*hand above head*), yeah? And the light's a bit murky? And the looters're back?

O'TOOLE: The what?

RYDER: He told me. These fuckers're after the goods, relics and shit . . . If we don't close this up for him before the next raid, the place'll be unguarded and his bollocks'll be in the mangle.

O'TOOLE: He told you this, Ryder Billy?

RYDER: I just told you. (*He comes up again, calls its number as he collects the block.*) Billy Ryder. Who knows the score. Makes it his business. Just don't go getting foolish on me, eh?

(RYDER *winks, his friend.* O'TOOLE *nods compliance.* RYDER *dips to lay the block;* O'TOOLE *dips to keep the stack three high.*) (*Up again; number over block.*) Make sense?

O'TOOLE: Can't fault it.

(*They go down again, up;* RYDER *calls the number, takes the block;* O'TOOLE *replaces.*)

RYDER: Still with me?

O'TOOLE: All the way, Billy Ryder. We'll drink to it. (*He moves off to fetch drink from his case.*) Stand by, my friend, you could be in for a real experience.

24

RYDER: (*Moving out*) I need a leak . . . Fags, I'm out . . .

O'TOOLE: Fags. Not a problem.

 (*He's reached the case, takes out a lemonade bottle half full of clear liquid, pouches it in his work robe, watches* RYDER *round the tent for his leak, pads silently across to the still-phoning* ISMAEL. *Inserts his shadow across the youth's face to announce his presence.* ISMAEL *blinks, swivels, sits up, stares; puts girlfriend on hold, coiled to act.*)

 (*In Arabic*) I come in peace.

ISMAEL: Go work. Fuck off.

O'TOOLE: Mr Ryder wondered if you might spare him a cigarette, he is without them . . .

ISMAEL: (*Handing pack*) Take. Skedaddle. (*He moves back to reconnect with his girl, sees* O'TOOLE *hasn't moved, fishing out one cigarette and returning the pack.*)

 What?

O'TOOLE: One's fine. Sufficient unto the day . . .

 (ISMAEL *returns to his call, only slowly realizes he's no longer connected.*)

 I pray the day confer success upon your endeavours, Ismael, son of Akram, brother of Saïd. I give you a charm for the journey, from the prophet Jeremiah. Life may indeed be just a bowl of cherries, you've still got to look out for the stones . . .

 (ISMAEL *curses in Arabic, waggles the phone around.* RYDER's *returning to the wall.* O'TOOLE *holds up the cigarette.*)

 (*Leaving*) I think you'll find that's the battery . . .

 (*He's gone.* ISMAEL *smacks the phone with his fist, pissed off.* RYDER's *laying, calling numbers.*)

 (*Back*) Here we go, pal. (*Pours tot into bottle cap.*) May the good Lord smile on our efforts.

RYDER: What is it?

O'TOOLE: This? Elixir of Life. Crushed velvet in the mouth. Poteen. (*Bottle up*) Slanje.

RYDER: (*Smelling it*) Smells like meths.

O'TOOLE: Drink. It'll help you with the pain. Success.

 (*They drink.* O'TOOLE *recaps the bottle, pouches it.*)

 Save the rest for the topping out, eh?

(*He checks out* ISMAEL, *who's occupied despatching a guard for new batteries. Resumes work.*)

RYDER: Pain? What pain?

O'TOOLE: What?

RYDER: You said it helps wi' the pain. I'm not in pain.

O'TOOLE: 'S just an expression. You know, like 'Here's mud in your eye' . . .

RYDER: You get the fags?

O'TOOLE: Oh aye. Fag actually. He's short. He's sendin' out for some . . .
(*He's fiddled the cigarette from his pocket, waits for* RYDER *to dip back from the stack to lay his next block.*)
(*Laying it on the top of the block stack*) There when you want it, Bill . . .

RYDER: (*A brief look, busy*) Right, I'll get it in a tick . . .
(O'TOOLE *calmly moves the cigarette along and down on to the block left uncovered by the block* RYDER's *now laying, talking as he monitors* RYDER's *progress.*)

O'TOOLE: Serendipity. Happy circumstance. You 'n' me meetin' up like this. (*The brick's almost laid.*) 'Long indeed is the day that does not have surprises in it.' Ezekiel.
(*He ducks down to gather a block, carefully angling to keep* RYDER *in peripheral vision.*
RYDER *stands, cleans his hands on his shorts, looks for the fag: no number. Checks* ISMAEL *out. Looks up at the sky.*)
(*Firming grip for the swing up*) You're goin' along, nothin' really happenin' for ye, then suddenly, outa the blue . . .

RYDER: (*Somewhere else*) Right, I'll have that fag . . .

O'TOOLE: (*Up and across, slams the block on to the reaching hand*) Bang!

RYDER: (*Huge*) JESUS . . . CHRIST.

O'TOOLE: (*Perfectly incredulous; horrified*) What happened?
(*A chaos of blocks and screams, oaths and recriminations spills across the site.* ISMAEL *legs over, yelling in Arabic. Militiamen run on, guns in hand.* RYDER *squirms and contorts his way around the place, somewhere between apeshit and agony.*
O'TOOLE *follows him around, trying to tend him.*)
(*Over and over*) Billy, how was I to know, you didn't call your

26

number, I'm truly sorry, what can I say . . .?

RYDER: (*More than once*) Just leave me alone, will ya, you're not safe . . .

ISMAEL: Hey. What's happening? Why you do this . . .?

O'TOOLE: Accident, friend. A brick trapped his fingers.

ISMAEL: Show. (*He squats over* RYDER.) Show.
(RYDER's *hand emerges from his belly.* ISMAEL *takes it gently in his own; they study the mess together.*)
Move.

RYDER: Shit.

ISMAEL: Move. (*Studies movement.*) No bones. It's good. You be OK?

RYDER: Yeah yeah . . .

ISMAEL: You finish wall in time?

RYDER: Yeah yeah, 's not the trowel hand . . . give us a minute or two.

ISMAEL: (*Reaching for it*) I take this . . .
(*He gathers one of the cotton gloves* RYDER *wears in his waistband.*)
What is it . . .?

O'TOOLE: Glove.
(ISMAEL *turns to look at him.*)

ISMAEL: Glove, yes. (*To* RYDER) Make you better.
(*He carries the glove away, searches for something in the rubble, eventually rounds the tent.* RYDER *lies back a bit, eyes closed, still in pain.*)

RYDER: I think I'm gonna be sick . . .

O'TOOLE: (*Eyes on sky to west*) Get it all up, son. (*Looks about him briefly.*) You're not likely to spoil aught.
(RYDER *looks across at him.*)

RYDER: (*Hard, mean; quite brutal*) I knew as soon as I clapped eyes on you, I'll tell, you thick Irish twat ye, Paddy, clumsy bogtrotting pig-ignorant get ye, we're fucked, thanks to you we are totally and comprehensively fucked, out of the goodness of my heart, did I need to? No way, I cut you in, you crush my fuckin' hand with a fuckin' breezeblock, is that life or is that, Jesus God, no wonder you dress like 'em, Seamus, you're exactly their fuckin' level.
(O'TOOLE *turns to look at him. Silence. Takes out a wallet,*

27

fiddles out a pad and pencil, rummages the wad.)
          (*Suddenly*) That's my wallet!
O'TOOLE: It is.
RYDER: What're you doing?
O'TOOLE: (*Preoccupied with wallet*) Just now I'm doing what I
          have to. And praying rather fiercely my eye doesn't wander
          from the ball.
          (*He pockets two hundred dinar, takes out an extraordinary
          contraption, multiple lenses set in a worked metal half-medieval
          headpiece, slips it on, lenses up, begins writing something in the
          pad.*)
RYDER: (*Slow*) You're mad. He is. O my God. O'Toole. O'Toole.
          Thinks he's Lawrence of whatsit. You're. Mad. (*He barks:*)
          Sun shrivelled the brain-pan.
O'TOOLE: Or. (*He writes on.*) What?
RYDER: You tell me.
O'TOOLE: When you need to know, if, then I'll tell you.
RYDER: Out of his tree.
          (O'TOOLE *folds the bills inside the note, pouches them. Stands to
          watch* ISMAEL *returning with the glove.*)
O'TOOLE: You listen but you don't hear, Ryder Billy. You look
          but you don't see. You've no smell so you can't taste. You
          speak but you don't mean. You touch but you can't feel.
          How shall we define this 'mad', Ryder Billy? Indeed, how
          shall we define major peckerhead? Sorry I had to whack you.
          I'm not fond of violence. You left me no option. A man who
          believes he knows the score is a desperate encumbrance.
          Particularly when he hasn't an inkling of the game he's in.
RYDER: (*Slow, low*) You. Cunt.
O'TOOLE: Warm, Ryder Billy. Friend Ismael . . .
ISMAEL: (*Kneeling*) Hand.
          (*He takes it gently, eases the cotton glove, wet and oozy now, on
          to the hand.*)
          How it feels, that?
RYDER: Aye. Not bad. Sorta warm. Mm. What is it?
ISMAEL: Old Bedouin doing.
RYDER: Ahunh.
ISMAEL: It's er pitch. And er . . . (*Looks for word again.*)

28

O'TOOLE: Piss.

(ISMAEL *turns again to stare at him*.)

ISMAEL: (*Smiles, shy*) Piss. Thank you.

RYDER: Yes, indeed.

(ISMAEL *stands. Scans the western sky. Isn't keen on what he's seeing*.)

ISMAEL: Half-hour, ten minutes, it's good, OK, tip-top, take easy, your man will do clunk splat . . .

RYDER: Yeah yeah. Absolutely.

ISMAEL: (*Stands; looks at* O'TOOLE) So. We build the wall.

O'TOOLE: That's the plan.

ISMAEL: Tick tick.

(*He's seen the militiaman returning with batteries and bars of chocolate. Heads for him. Sits to eat his chocs and reactivate phone.* O'TOOLE *gathers a new can of Stone's, takes out the note and bills*.)

RYDER: (*Bleak, dark; some fear there*) I don't get you. I don't get you at all. What sort of a man, eh, cold-bloodedly and by design, eh? Tell me. In words of one syllable: what game on? What're you playin' for? I want out, I've been honest with you. What do *you* want? I've a right, in common decency, in the same shitheap, to some fuckin' answers.

(O'TOOLE *stoops, picks something up from the sand by* RYDER's *feet. Stands with it. It's the cigarette, crushed and bent*.)

O'TOOLE: Done for. I must cadge you another.

(*He pads off, headed for* ISMAEL, *who's getting someone to call him, checking the bell*.)

RYDER: (*After him*) O'Toole. You are definitely on my shitlist.

O'TOOLE: Mine too.

(ISMAEL *sees him coming, cuts call, stands, arms folded, to watch him in, forces him to talk from below him*.)

ISMAEL: What? Get lost. You walk around, build the goddamn wall, you say nothing I wish to hear, you know the time. . . .?

O'TOOLE: I do. It's time to cut the crap, Ismael, son of Ahram, brother of Saïd. The schoolboy who played wag to come to the Winter Palace with a football under his arm to strut his

29

stuff before the infidel workers and the talks he'd hang on for with O'Toole the Gilder . . . Mm? The man who taught you how to bring a ball down on your instep?

ISMAEL: O'Toole. Cut the crap. I know this story. Once I was a child. Today, this day, you deal with a man . . . The rest is bullshits . . .

O'TOOLE: Just so. OK. Simply stated, you're fucked. The facts. You'll be lucky if Ryder can reach 25 per cent of laying speed. He's not good with pain. Plus your confidence in my building prowess is wholly misplaced. I am a master gilder, the builder on my I.D. is a typographical error, a master gilder does not build walls. I'm hoping you're right about being a man, Ismael, there's choices to be made, it'll take a man . . .

ISMAEL: A man serves his country and his people. When a man treads into choices, he calls his Major . . .

O'TOOLE: Even when he knows he'd be safer slashing his own throat? Here. (*Hands him note and bills*.) You can phone the Major or build the wall, not both. This man is a layer, I know him a little, he's available, that's where he's staying. Call this guy, right, Case Officer, the dinars are a present for his son's wedding, he'll see he's bussed over, you get your wall, the Major saves his skin, buries whatever it is, Christ knows what, you can smell it, it's everywhere, and no Ministry in sight, keeping it local. You've about (*Looks at sky, at watch*) no time at all. Make the right call, eh?

(*He leaves.* ISMAEL *sniffs. Spits.*)

ISMAEL: Why? What's for you in this, O'Toole?

O'TOOLE: (*Going on*) The pleasure of helping friends. The satisfaction of thwarting an enemy or two. All the old bullshit.

ISMAEL: Bullshit, sure. Hey, this I handle, you think I don't have the bottles? Fuck you.

(O'TOOLE *heads back for the prone* RYDER, *who whimpers, sleeping.*

ISMAEL *paces and frets about the ridge, dealing with crisis. Looks up suddenly; the pall thickens again, the air dims. He hurls an instruction down to the truck, a voice answers.*

He sits. Takes out the phone. Studies the note, face vacant, digging deep.

30

O'TOOLE *sits by the sleeping* RYDER. *Gathers a pair of pebbles, bangs them rhythmically together, swaying a little.* RYDER *wakes, turns, stares at* O'TOOLE.)

RYDER: 'S happenin'?

O'TOOLE: He's sendin' for the brickie.

(RYDER *turns on his other side to look.* ISMAEL *sits immobile, the phone pouched.*)

RYDER: How do you know?

(ISMAEL *stands, takes out the phone, keys out a number, disappears over the rubble ridge as the call connects.*)

O'TOOLE: He's got no choice.

(*Militiamen move up, lit paraffin lamps in their hands, begin rigging them about the work area.*
Music; low.
Very slow creep up, houselights.
RYDER *gets to his feet, peels off the glove, moves gingerly over to the work site area, working the damaged mitt.*)

RYDER: I'm gonna see what I can do, if that's all right.

O'TOOLE: Need a hand?

RYDER: Thanks. I have one.

(*A muezzin sets up. His voice washes the site. The Ancients lay down their long shovels, wash in the burst-main pool, approach the forestage, turn towards Mecca to worship.*
Houselights on.
RYDER *builds painfully, drives himself a bit, in a sort of dull rage. He brings the wall to perhaps five courses before pain and fatigue lay him out.*
O'TOOLE *half helps, half wanders, checking out. Mixes more mortar.*
The Ancients finish their worship, squat in the sand to eat their snap, make music with tabla and oud, leading to dance.
The wall crawls upward. RYDER *rests the hand a lot.* ISMAEL *reappears, goes again, phone at ear. Later, a call from perimeter fence; he answers, leaves.*
Houselights eventually to slow fade. The site's weirdly dark, the lamps bright.)

31

ACT TWO

The Ancients have returned to their recovery work among the rubble. One of them has left the site; returns with a wheelbarrow; snails his way with it across the wasteland to rejoin his comrade.

RYDER has rounded the tented shrine to take a piss. He's not in good shape.

O'TOOLE climbs a fragment of rubbled building, stoops to gather the bus-driver's cap, stares at it a moment as his gilder's spot glows in on him.

O'TOOLE: (*Narrative voice*) The dance was real. It happened. Yet it was not written; rather the dance wrote itself. Rose up from the sand, already inside these unrecorded peasants, and brought the foreigners gently to their senses, stilled time itself, wrought place anew, shared out joy and ease in common purpose, stopped the sun in its tracks, to cancel the coming slaughter. But the music died; and the day and the war – the Grand and the Petty – resumed their customary clamour. Voices, questions, ifs and buts, echoed round his brain-pan: had he the story aright, would the young Minder risk all for all and have the Apprentice brought, to give his plans for rescue the chance to prosper? Would the battered Builder fall in line or splinter underfoot like brushwood, most of all, would the Gilder's own failing memory and crumbling eyesight last the journey? The waiting minutes slid away as he reviewed the possible outcomes and his joy was very far from unconfined. But honour held him fast, he told himself, he had given the Apprentice's family his solemn word he would be cared for, no master leaves his pupil in the lurch, etc. Besides, one should in truth add, the Gilder well knew how bleak his own future as a craftsman would be without him. Madness Rafael might have by the bucketful, but there was method in there too . . .
(*The spot dies, the remains of the day struggle to reassert against the gloom.*

32

*Guards push on a young Indian, T-shirt and shorts, chained
hand and foot, a hood tied on his head.*

O'TOOLE *turns, sees* RYDER, *returned from his pee, staring at
the chained and hooded prisoner.*)

RYDER: I don't believe this . . .

O'TOOLE: What?

RYDER: You've had him send for a *Gaol*bird . . .?

O'TOOLE: You will rush to judgement, Billy . . .

RYDER: He's in chains, for God's sake . . .

O'TOOLE: He's being held on suspicion, a minor infraction, no
evidence, a trumped-up charge, rozzers're the same the
world over, the boy's blameless . . .

RYDER: (*Distinct*) He's a *prisoner*, O'Toole. That means I'm
gonna have a gun trained on me the whole time he's here
. . . (*Looks at sky.*) I'm going to die. It's certain.
(RYDER *shivers, begins to wander downstage, face bleak, feet
aimless, headed for the perimeter tape.* O'TOOLE *watches.*)
I'm cold. (*Rubs himself.*) Is it cold?

O'TOOLE: Don't ask me. I'm always cold.
(O'TOOLE *collects a garment from Ryder's bags, eyes fixed on
the wandering* RYDER.)
Billy . . .

RYDER: Can't hear you.

O'TOOLE: No exit, Billy.

RYDER: Can't hear you.

O'TOOLE: You won't die.

RYDER: Can't hear you.

O'TOOLE: It isn't written.
(RYDER *stops abruptly, drops into a kneeling slouch in the
sand. Stares out, fingers joined at lap.*)

RYDER: Fuck off.
(O'TOOLE *carries a jacket over. Lays it gently over* RYDER's
*shoulders. Ryder scarcely notices, his lips moving on a prayer
that won't form.*)

O'TOOLE: (*Squatting; mouth to ear*) It's in hand. This time
tomorrow you're poolside at the Cairo Hilton, this time
next week you'll be on *Wogan*, an overnight hero, millions
of small businessmen the length and breadth of Britain

hanging on your every whopper. Trust me.

(ISMAEL *yells at the guards, on the return.* O'TOOLE *stands, lays a hand on* RYDER's *shoulder.*)

My hand, my word.

ISMAEL: (*Pumped up*) Give me your name. I want your name. O'Toole!

(O'TOOLE *moves off up the rubble slope towards the group around the prisoner.*

RYDER's *hand moves slowly up to cover the touched shoulder, his desperate loneliness for a moment palpable. Somewhere inside the pain of things, his fingers recognize the Armani.*)

RYDER: Oh Christ. Not my best suit.

(*He looks down. The hem trails in oil-soaked sand.*

On the ridge, the guards are removing the wrist irons; Ismael questions the still-hooded prisoner, his details on a card in his hand.)

ISMAEL: (*To* O'TOOLE) This guy don't hear me, he deaf, mister . . .?

O'TOOLE: (*Stopping halfway*) Try losing the hood.

(ISMAEL *sniffs. Begins unfastening the tie-cord.*)

(*To prisoner*) Welcome to the nursery, Chatty. Today we're building a wall.

(*A mangled phrase from beneath the hood: possibly 'Fuck off, O'Toole.'*)

Remember Habbakuk: 'Silence is golden.' All will be revealed.

(*The hood comes off. The young Asian, twenty-five or so, blinks a scan of the place, ends with a heavy glare at* O'TOOLE *down the slope.*)

ISMAEL: (*From card*) Chatterjee Anand, yes?

O'TOOLE: Correct.

ISMAEL: Builder, yes?

(*The Asian glares again at* O'TOOLE.)

O'TOOLE: Definitely.

ISMAEL: Why he don't answer? He deaf, yes?

O'TOOLE: He's dumb.

ISMAEL: What 'dumb'?

O'TOOLE: Mute. (*Gives the word in Arabic.*) Someone accidentally

34

ran a laser through his larynx, back in wherever it is he comes from. He thought of reporting it to the authorities, but since the accident took place in a police cell, he decided not to pursue the matter . . .

(ISMAEL *stares hard at* O'TOOLE, *sniffing for treacheries. A sudden braying chuckle from* RYDER *down below, on his feet again, taking it all in.*)

What's the problem, he's here to lay bricks for your sweating Major, not seduce us with his oratory . . .

ISMAEL: Shut up your trap, gilder! (*To Chatterjee*) OK, you do clunk splat, you do it fast, we get the fucker done . . .

(*He growls instructions, the guards push Chatterjee towards the shrine.* O'TOOLE *stays put.*)

(*Calling*) We work, Ryder Billy, you too, you see this one do good, OK?

RYDER: (*Oddly buckshee*) Putty in your hands, *mein Führer*.

ISMAEL: (*To* O'TOOLE) Hey. You too.

O'TOOLE: What about his legs, Ismael, how's he gonna . . . ?

ISMAEL: I tell you once, I tell you twice, your boy fuck around I blow them off.

(O'TOOLE *sniffs, turns to leave.*)

Major's orders.

(*Silence.*)

O'TOOLE: I thought we'd put the Major behind us, Ismael.

ISMAEL: My Major knows everything. You think I'm crazy? He fix this, no problem.

(*A guard calls from the women's perimeter.* ISMAEL *swings round to look, sees* DR AZIZ *headed slowly up towards the site.*)

O'TOOLE: (*Dealing with the news*) Your Major's in deeper shit than I thought.

ISMAEL: Hey. Maybe you don't notice, British, we fight a war here . . .

(*He barks instructions down to the two guards at the shrine, wheels off along the ridge to confront the approaching woman. The guards unsling their Stens, retreat to vantage points – the ridge, the forestage perimeter – to cover the workers.*

O'TOOLE *watches* ISMAEL *and* DR AZIZ *begin low-pitched exchange for a moment, then pads back to the shrine.* RYDER'*s slipped into his jacket, arrives ahead of him.*)

RYDER: Hi, welcome to the nuthouse. Name's Ryder. Billy.

CHATTERJEE: (*Hand out*) Yow yu.

(RYDER *gingerly offers his own, wipes it on his shorts, a largely unconscious gesture.*)

RYDER: Sorry about the er . . .

(*He indicates throat.* CHATTERJEE *nods.* RYDER *hands him his trowel.*)

We've less than an hour, I hope you're fast . . .

O'TOOLE: (*Returning, businesslike*) Forget it, Bill, he's no more a brickie than I am, just another typo . . . Now, for God's sake, look handy, will you . . . More mortar, Billy . . . Chatty, give 'and wi' this . . .

(*He begins assembling the crude scaffolding ready for the higher courses.* CHATTERJEE *clanks over to help, seriously angry yowls escaping from his clenched teeth.*)

RYDER: (*Distinct*) What did you say?

(O'TOOLE *waves him quiet, eyes fixed on the meeting on the ridge as he works on. The talk is low-toned, rational, but* ISMAEL *has kept* DR AZIZ *at the bottom of the far slope, still not on the site proper.*)

O'Toole?

O'TOOLE: (*Working, watching*) This may come as a bit of a blow, Ryder Billy, but I've not been entirely honest with you up to now.

CHATTERJEE: Yyin yun.

O'TOOLE: Dummy up, kid. It's in hand.

(*He looks at* RYDER, *who's going crazy with the mortar.*)

This is not the moment to freak out, Billy . . .

RYDER: I can't hear you, you're gone, ppp, you're a loony, whatever you've got in that horrible . . . diseased . . . bent brain of yours, sorry, can't hear you . . . WHO'S GONNA BUILD THE FUCKING WALL?

(ISMAEL *turns to look briefly at the builders, returns to the troublesome* DR AZIZ.)

O'TOOLE: (*Toneless; deeply calm*) I'm coming to that, Bill. OK?

RYDER: Can't hear you, sorry.

(DR AZIZ *crests the ridge. Ismael's hand moves inside his coat, falls clear.* O'TOOLE *watches and listens.*)

ISMAEL: (*In Arabic*) I have my orders . . .

DR AZIZ: (*In Arabic*) What is the problem? It will take a couple of minutes, and I can also send the women home happy before the bombs start falling . . .

ISMAEL: (*In Arabic*) The Major's orders are explicit . . .

DR AZIZ: (*In Arabic; tough*) Then call the Major. Report the problem. He will understand, I promise you.

(*A small stand-off.* ISMAEL *yanks the phone out, keys a number.* DR AZIZ *waits for connection, picks her way down the rubble. Stands below in silence, trying not to stare at the shrine, a fret of concern worrying her lips.*)

O'TOOLE: (*Watching*) Building the wall's not a problem, Chat can do a bit, I can do a bit, you can do a bit, I mean we're not after an RIBA award or aught, are we . . . The problem now is timing . . .

RYDER: Lost you again, sorry . . . I think I'd better have a word with friend Ismael.

(*He stands.* O'TOOLE *nods to* CHATTERJEE. *Ryder takes a pace, the Indian's big hand noiselessly arrests his forward motion by the scruff of the neck.*)

All right, all right, all right. What's the plan then?

(CHATTERJEE's *hand relaxes.*)

Gonna call a chopper in, fly us all out, that'd be good, that'd get my vote, definitely.

(O'TOOLE *scans the ridge.* ISMAEL *stamps along it and back, phone to ear, on hold, waiting for the Major's meeting to finish.* He looks across at DR AZIZ. *She's staring at him, half reproach, half entreaty, the tugs powerful for both of them. He pulls away, an act of will, fixes on* RYDER.)

O'TOOLE: Timing, Billy. Between the siren and the raid. We finish the wall. That's the only chance this poor afflicted bastard has of flying the coop . . .

(ISMAEL's *voice, low, urgent; he's through.* O'TOOLE *checks* DR AZIZ. *She's turned to watch* ISMAEL; *turns again to return his gaze.*)

(*Soft; inward*) God's wounds. This was also written. I remember me . . .

37

RYDER: What about *this* poor afflicted bastard (*himself*), O'Toole?

O'TOOLE: She says . . .

DR AZIZ: (*Seamlessly; low across the space*) Might I have a word, please?

RYDER: (*Clenched teeth*) I have my papers, I wanna be in a shelter when that fuckin' siren goes, not arsin' about helpin' your Paki friend skip . . .

CHATTERJEE: (O'TOOLE's *voice*) He says . . .

O'TOOLE: (*Across the space*) With you directly, doctor.

RYDER: Who said that?

O'TOOLE: I did.

RYDER: (*Looking from one to the other*) Oh God, I know what you are, you're special, oh my God, you're special ops, aren't you, you're . . .

O'TOOLE: Ryder. I'm just me. Rafael Finbar O'Toole, the Wandering Gilder. Trying to survive in rather difficult times. Praying the Good Doctor does not blow us off course . . . Trust me. Build.

(*He slaps the scaffolding section he's just finished. Sees* ISMAEL *finish the call and house the phone. Heads for the woman, collects the bus-driver's cap as he goes. A slow rhythmic handclap sets up from the women's perimeter. A cry from a guard: the women are* back. ISMAEL *yells at the onsite guards, the man on the ridge heads off for the women's perimeter, the other takes his place on the ridge.* ISMAEL *calls reinforcements up from the men's perimeter.*)

(*Stopped, some way from her*) Can I help?

DR AZIZ: I need to make a brief inspection. I have to file a report for the Department. An inventory . . .

(O'TOOLE *nods, scans the rubble. An Ancient empties his full bin-liner into the wheelbarrow.*)

O'TOOLE: You should speak with the men here, they're gathering . . .

DR AZIZ: In there, I mean.

(*He looks at her, turns, stares at the shrine.* RYDER *and* CHATTERJEE *have laboriously begun the next course.*)

RYDER: (*Reasserting*) No no, for Christ's sake, *this* way, right . . .?

O'TOOLE: The shrine?

38

DR AZIZ: The crèche.

(*Silence. Guards pour across to the women's perimeter. A rhythmic chanting builds around the handclaps.*)

O'TOOLE: (*Lost*) The crèche.

DR AZIZ: The shrine became a mosque, the mosque a crèche, in this part of the world we learn to nurse our resources . . . Perhaps you would ask your men to stop, I shouldn't be long . . .

O'TOOLE: What about him?

DR AZIZ: (*Looking across at* ISMAEL) He's checking with his superior. He's a boy. He should be playing football, learning a skill . . .

(O'TOOLE *nods, turns towards the shrine, looks back at* DR AZIZ.)

O'TOOLE: Talking to the mothers didn't help, hunh?

DR AZIZ: What do you mean?

(O'TOOLE *stares on at her.*)

O'TOOLE: I'm not certain I can afford to care about this. I am, as they say, powerless to help. But if you're going to make an inspection and file a report, you're going to have to do it unauthorized, you're not stupid or naïve enough to believe the Major and his handlers will say, 'Stop building, let her proceed.' The Major will say . . .

ISMAEL: (*In Arabic; calling, headed down slope, jacket in hand*) You will report to your superior, they're sending a car, the work has priority . . .

(*He slides, loses balance, pitches forward, his jacket arm plunging into standing water. He curses, scrabbles in pockets, fishes out the dripping phone, moves doggedly on, shaking as he goes.*)

O'TOOLE: Your boss wants to see you, they're sending a car, build the wall . . . Take a look. (*He nods at her to look at the sprawled minder.*) This good soldier is not a well human being. Half of him's a pistol on legs, half's all at sea. How important can it *be* to make an inventory of a burnt-out shell? A thousand gallons of fuel burning at fifteen hundred degrees, what d'you think's gonna be left? In the meantime . . .

ISMAEL: (*Limping up; in Arabic*) In the meantime, you will go

39

down to the perimeter and reassure the unruly women you
have seen with your own eyes, their fears are groundless . . .

O'TOOLE: Your orders are to lie to the women. End of story.

(ISMAEL *frowns a look across at* O'TOOLE, *who twiddles the
found cap in his fingers.*)

Builder says . . .

RYDER: (*Calling*) Could we have a ruling over here, please?

(*He's trying to help* CHATTERJEE *climb the scaffolding, the
leg-irons the problem.*)

I mean, either he keeps these buggers on or we can build the
wall . . . I mean it's up to you, boss, but I *am* a builder, I do
know about these things . . .

ISMAEL: OK, I look at. (*To* DR AZIZ; *in Arabic*) You go, Dr
Fadia, it's best for all . . .

RYDER: Take your time, we've got minutes and minutes . . .

ISMAEL: (*Arabic*) The only thing these women have to fear is their
own frenzy driving them to interfere with our work here, for
then they will surely get hurt, I cannot disobey my
orders . . .

(DR AZIZ *blinks. Bites her lip. Searches for an answer. Pulls her
headshawl tighter.*)

Excuse me, ma'am . . .

(*He heads off for the wall. Sizes up the problem. Eventually
begins unkeying the leg-irons.*)

O'TOOLE: (*Climbing to look at the women's perimeter*) Don't even
think about it. He had the Shias mown down for trying to
stop them violating their ancient shrine with unclean labour,
the women'll go the same way . . . As it happens, you do not
even have to lie, there really is nothing to see in there to
cause them concern, I've seen it for myself, inspected it
earlier, what you have basically is the inside of a large
Tandoori oven . . . no desks, no tables, no soft toys, no hard
toys, no chairs, no wall-paintings, no gilt. Ash. Bitumen.
End of inventory.

DR AZIZ: (*Low; unable to complete*) No . . .?

O'TOOLE: A. B. No C.

DR AZIZ: Can I believe you?

O'TOOLE: Do I look like a liar?

DR AZIZ: If liars looked like liars, who would believe them?

ISMAEL: (*Fierce, sudden call*) O'Toole, over here, now . . .

O'TOOLE: Yessir!

(*He shrugs, peels away, rejoining the wall group.*
DR AZIZ stands on; turns sharply; heads eventually for the
women's perimeter.
Her subsequent address to the mothers persists for much of the
sequence that follows and, even at distance, remains in tone and
content audible and intelligible throughout. It culminates in
shouted expressions of gratitude, deep relief and praise to Allah;
and eventual dispersal.
ISMAEL has freed the Indian's legs; ordered RYDER and
CHATTERJEE to resume building.)

ISMAEL: OK, O'Toole, better we talk . . .

RYDER: Better we build this bloody thing, Ismael. O'Toole,
thirty more blocks, mek it forty, let's go . . .

(O'TOOLE *calls the Ancients in Arabic. Looks at* ISMAEL.)

ISMAEL: Two minutes.

(*He points where, wanders up there, shaking the phone, needing*
it to work. Crosses to the ruined hulk, looks down towards the
women's perimeter, listens, stone-faced, blank-eyed, to
DR AZIZ's *address.*
O'TOOLE *gets the old guys cracking. Looks up at* RYDER *who's*
painfully pulled himself up on to the scaffolding to join
CHATTERJEE *laying.*)

O'TOOLE: Bill.

RYDER: (*Routine*) Fuck off.

O'TOOLE: The story. We're still workin', nearly there, the
secret's all but buried, right? The siren goes. Thirty seconds
later . . . at the most . . . I've *seen* these boys shift for that
shelter . . . it's just Ismael and us.

RYDER: I'd say we were still heavily outnumbered.

O'TOOLE: Thirty seconds after that, it's just Ismael and me,
you're off to the shelter, next the world . . . You hearing me
yet?

RYDER: (*Deliberate*) I have. My papers. O'Toole. Even if you
manage to stop me leaving tonight, I can leave. Tomorrow.

O'TOOLE: Oh dear. If you believe that, Billy, you'll believe . . .

(*He shakes his head, peels away.*)

RYDER: (*After him*) Hey, pull the other one, I showed 'em to you, you seem t'forget that . . .

(O'TOOLE *pads away towards* ISMAEL *up at the watch-post.*
DR AZIZ *is winding up, the women begin to respond.*
RYDER *watches* O'TOOLE *for some moments, face puckering as he begins to suspect faulty reasoning somewhere. Turns to find* CHATTERJEE *staring at him and shaking his head in contemptuous disbelief, there well ahead of him.*)

He's lying, right?

CHATTERJEE: Uhunh.

RYDER: He's lying. I'm telling you.

(*They return to laying.* RYDER *repeats* 'He's lying' *as he works.*
CHATTERJEE *drops in a few* 'Uhunhs' *and a* 'Yo-yay', *to stir the pot.*)

O'TOOLE: Last orders, friend.

(ISMAEL *swivels to face him, eyes dark.* O'TOOLE *holds out his passport.*)

Save your breath.

ISMAEL: (*Taking it*) How you know this?

O'TOOLE: It was in your eyes. And I'd read the book. (*Hands him I.D.*) And I.D.? Of course.

(O'TOOLE *sits to face the city.* ISMAEL *calls the remaining guard over, gives him the papers, mutters instructions, the guy heads off.*)

(*Throughout*) I've been minded all my working life, Ismael, across Africa, Asia, South America, wherever I can find some appalling little shite in a crown, some beast in a beret, some ermined vermin with power to spare and the desire to indulge a passion for giltwork, minders and gold-leaf, it's all I've known. Was it not the holy Balalah, the Prophet's uncle, who said, 'The mind of the minder is as an open sewer ateem with the crimes of obedience, on which only the pure of heart may gaze, and then only if they can handle the stench' . . .?

(*The Ancients trundle in with their block-laden barrows. The wall-builders work on in muttery silence.*
Sounds of the women dispersing, calls in the evening streets.
O'TOOLE *turns, sees* ISMAEL *eyeing him, the papers despatched.*)

42

You wanted to talk.

ISMAEL: It's done. (*Hands* O'TOOLE *his own note from Act One.*) We fix the wall, we get the prisoner back to police cell, same man returns your documents . . . I send them bye bye.
(*He chuckles, pleased at the neatness.* O'TOOLE *stands, chuckles with him.*)

O'TOOLE: Nice one, friend. You'll make major yet, you see.
(*He lays down the driver's cap very carefully on a slab of rubble. Pulls the mesh of scorched cable from the roof out of his tunic, lays it carefully beside the cap.*)

ISMAEL: What you have here?

O'TOOLE: One cap, peaked, bus drivers for the use of, City Transport Department (Schools). One length of coaxial cable, from a concreted gully let in to the roof of the holy place there . . .

ISMAEL: You're crazy, man. You walk about, you talk, it's not good, why you bring this crap . . .?

O'TOOLE: I was hoping you'd tell me, Ismael.

ISMAEL: Hey. What you know?
(*Silence. A guard calls something up from the women's perimeter.*)

RYDER: (*Slumping back on scaffold*) That's me. I'm fucked.
(*A car arriving, women's perimeter, siren blaring.* ISMAEL *flicks a look.*)

O'TOOLE: Exit the Good Doctor.
(DR AZIZ *enters as if on cue, at the side of the tented shrine. She stands, back against wall, drawing breath, shielded from the site by the building. She's drained; not sure what she's doing; slides to a squat, back to the wall.*
Raised voices from the perimeter, shouts, a guard struggles up to speak with ISMAEL.
O'TOOLE *waits until he knows enough, returns to the wall area, opens a can of beer, hands it up to the knackered* RYDER. *Serious hoo-haa develops around the site, calls in Arabic for* DR AZIZ *to make her way to the women's perimeter, the car is waiting . . . A couple of dogs join the search. Pressure builds on* ISMAEL; *a second guard moves in, the minder sent to escort* DR AZIZ *wants him down at the car right away. He calls up two men to cover the builders, eventually heads off at speed.*)

43

Through this –
O'TOOLE *goes to sit beneath the scaffolding, his back to the wall edge, all but visible to the now seated* DR AZIZ.)
(*Remote; inturned*) Ease down, Chatty.

RYDER: (*Gas gone*) Pay him no heed. He's all self, that one.
(CHATTERJEE *reaches for the can, dowses his head, drinks, stares, scans the city, the sky above it. Smiles, a seraph.*)

CHATTERJEE: (O'TOOLE's *voice*) There y'are, y'old bugger, off ter bed, is it . . .?
(*Pale intense light bursts slowly across the site, turning it spectral, on the edge of Magritte, the sky wholly black, the earth and brick vivid, unearthly, as the sinking sun shafts in from below the smoke pall.*
The four watch it in their separate silences.)
(*Vera Lynn's voice; a soft croon*)
> There'll be bluebirds over
> The white cliffs of Dover
> Tomorrow is another day.
(*Silence.*)

RYDER: How d'ye *do* that, O'Toole?

O'TOOLE: It's uncanny, innit, I know. I suppose it's a gift.

RYDER: 'S the story?
(*They listen: men, calls, dogs; the attention of the men covering the site already sucked to the search.*)

O'TOOLE: Time you got, Billy?

RYDER: Stopped. Thanks a bunch, Rolex.

O'TOOLE: (*Taking waterproof package from tunic*) The woman's done a runner, the heavies've arrived to drive her to a place of unsafety, she very sagely decided to hop it . . . Nice one, doc. (*Checks watch. Gathers pace.*) It'll be about a brick a minute, lads, rough guide, no more than six or eight left on the siren, I'll tek them, you'll wait for Chat, Ryder, he'll show you where, I'll join up with you at the river . . .
(*He's removed three passports from the waterproof, studies them, lens-crown on.* RYDER *angles from above to get a look at him.*)

RYDER: What's that?

O'TOOLE: Just sorting out a couple passports, just in case, Chatty's without, the little bugger just took mine . . . Right,

44

give it a bit o' welly, Chat, look handy . . .

(*A glance up at* RYDER *who's levering himself up for work.*)

This time we'll slip out the back door, so we won't need 'em
. . . Getting into the next place, who knows, maybe it'll be
easier goin' through the front . . . Aught else?

(*He stands, restows the gear, stretches.*)

RYDER: One question, O'Toole . . .

DR AZIZ: (*Quiet; distinct*) May I speak, please?

(*Silence. No one moves.*)

RYDER: Who said that?

O'TOOLE: (*Scanning the guards*) She did.

DR AZIZ: Will you hear me?

(RYDER, *then* CHATTERJEE, *stare into the shrine, tracing the
voice.*)

O'TOOLE: (*Soft*) This is not written.

DR AZIZ: I have no wish to be a bother to you. But you must
understand it is my intention . . .

O'TOOLE: Too late for new pages.

DR AZIZ: . . . to carry out an inspection of my crèche before I leave
this place.

RYDER: Crèche? 'S she talkin' ab –?

DR AZIZ: Not because I believe I sent the mothers off with a lie.
But because I cannot know the truth unless I see for myself.
These are not small things I speak of, gentlemen. Breach of
trust. The responsibilities of care. Mothers and children . . .

O'TOOLE: (*Shaking head*) Oh shit. (*He turns to the shrine.*) Let's get
this over. Chatty, let that flap down, son, we'll be blinded
else . . .

RYDER: The sun's over 'ere, what're you . . .? Hey, give your brain
a rest, O'Toole, no one goes in here, we let this one, this place
is gonna turn into a rifle range and we're right in fronta the
butts. You're GONNA GET ME KILLED, O'TOOLE. Fuck you
. . . I say we call Ismael, right now . . .

(CHATTERJEE *brings the flap down in a great sweep across the top
of the scaffolding, blocking eyelines for the guards on the ridge.*
DR AZIZ *has levered herself upright. Neatens her dress into some
kind of order.* RYDER's *voice has drawn a couple of them out of the
search and back to the site.*)

O'TOOLE: (*Over shoulder, light, casual*) You're such a prick, Ryder. It's breathtaking. It's in the voice, man, this is a woman in the act of drawing a line, she won't be deflected this side of paradise. So. Time could suddenly grow very short if this . . . spreads, right? She slips in, she slips out, two minutes, she's gone . . . (*He carries the tunic back to the scaffolding, drapes it, another screen, to dry.*) Call Ismael, this could outlast the war. What do I know, I'm making this up . . . (*He moves to look directly at* DR AZIZ *down the side of the shrine.*) My mistake. I remembered you as a doctor. I should've remembered you as a woman. See for yourself. If you must.

(*She walks past him with care, enters the shrouded passage, finds the steps to the scaffold,* CHATTERJEE *helping.*

RYDER *edges around the site, hand hurting, looking for ways of not dying if she's spotted.*

O'TOOLE *returns to the crater, squats before it, checks watch, sky. Stares into the water. A faint gold glow strikes up at his face from the pool, turning it ghastly. The glow comes and goes, like his fragmenting narrative. Shouts echo around the site. The sun's on a slow dip; reddening.*)

(*Blank*) Gilder Builder Minder Soldier Major
   Caliph Wall War Play Lamp Crown
   Prisoner Doctor . . .
(*Tries again.*)
   Doctor . . .
   He had not lied, he told himself.
   Lying.
   Between the alarm and the attack
   Between the heart and the brain-pan
   Between us the Gulf . . .
   The dark.
   Two minutes, in and out, the barn would be repaired, they
      would gain their release . . .
   Long ago, on an arch in the great Alhambra, he had
      written in letters of gold the words of Gilgamesh, king
      of the first city, builder of the first wall:
   Be what you are. Seek not what you may not find. Let

46

your every day be full of joy. Love the child that holds
your hand. Let your wife delight in your embrace. For
these alone are the concerns of humanity.

And now, the dark.

Half blind. Half gone in the head. Half . . .

(*Ululations set up abruptly, single voices, tiny clusters, this time
out front. The pool lamp flickers out.* O'TOOLE *stares at the city.*
ISMAEL *barks instructions, on the approach. The sentries turn to
see him in. He's telling them to help in the search; they slither
away.*)

ISMAEL: You finished, Ryder Billy?

RYDER: (*Edging back towards shrine*) All but, chief.

O'TOOLE: (*Calling*) How we doin', Chat? Almost ready to unveil?

(CHATTERJEE *moves into vision, downstage end of scaffolding,
waves his trowel, smiling benignly. The women's calls lift, grow
more intense.*)

ISMAEL: Show. Uncover.

(CHATTERJEE *doesn't move.*)

Ryder Billy! Do it.

RYDER *looks at* O'TOOLE, *begins to haul the canvas back and up
from the scaffolded wall. Several blocks have been picked out from
lower courses, to ease her entry.* ISMAEL *moves a pace or two
forward.* O'TOOLE *stands.*)

(*Slow*) What you do here? (*Scans the three.*) What the story?
O'Toole?

O'TOOLE: The story. Let me think . . .

(*A strange unearthly sound begins to build from within the shrine:
dog breath, shrieks of infants, the crack of burning bone. The
calling women fall abruptly silent. The site reddens, sun dipping
on. At the heart of the sound,* DR AZIZ's *voice, a growing
wretched terrifying wail, outlasting the rest.*
Silence.
ISMAEL *edges forward. Stops at movement beyond the wall.
Militiamen begin to appear on the ridge.* ISMAEL *sends them away.*
DR AZIZ *returns through the gap in the wall, her headshawl
bundled around something in her hands.*)

ISMAEL: (*In Arabic throughout*) Put it back. You put that back,
that's an order.

47

(He opens his jacket. DR AZIZ *looks at him steadily.)*

DR AZIZ: *(In Arabic)* May God forgive you, Ismael. *(She scans the three workers; in English)* May God forgive you too. *(A glance out front.)* May God forgive us all . . .

(She heads for the crater. Reaches ISMAEL. *He stands for some moments, turns abruptly away, goes back to his perch on the hulk above the site, stares out towards the perimeter.*

O'TOOLE *sits on the rubble ridge, face blank, in the dark.)*

O'TOOLE'S VOICE: *(Relay)* The bits we never remember. The bits we edit . . . out.

(DR AZIZ has sat by the pool. Rocks a bit, the bundle held close to her breast.

A single mother's voice, close, awful, calls her child's name: Ibrahim.)

DR AZIZ: Al-Aker. Ibrahim. Three years four months. *(To the sky beyond the city)* Who do you think you are? Mm? Who do you think we are?

(She lays the shawl down on earth. Unwraps it. Examines the contents.)

Perhaps. How can we tell?

(A second mother calls a name: Hanin.

On the shawl, an almost abstract shine-black sculpture of abbreviated limbs and torsos fused and reworked under intense heat, gleams on the cloth.)

Al-Kurdi. Hanin. Four. Recently recovered from dysentery. *(To sky)* What have we *done* to you, mm? What awful wrong? That you would kill children . . .? *(To the charcoal)* Hanin, is it? What shall I write in my report . . .?

MOTHER'S VOICES: Mamdouh. Waseem. Fadia. Eman. Shamma'eh . . .

DR AZIZ: *(To sky)* I have travelled in your countries, taken food in your homes, shared feelings and hopes, thought of you as brothers and sisters in the long struggle for human dignity. And I have seen you, Mr President, with your sensitive expression and sorrowing eyes on my television screen . . . And I had forgotten, what you will not acknowledge but the world knows, that yours is a country forged and shaped in brutal genocide, the destruction of whole peoples, lives,

48

customs, beliefs, men, women and children who had learned respect for the place that nourished them, who had learned to tread gently on this good earth . . .

A WOMAN'S VOICE: (*A child's name*) Ghazi.

DR AZIZ: (*To sky still*) You destroy your past with these acts. Your future too. Wars only have beginnings. No endings.

ANOTHER VOICE: (*Another child*) Samzi.

DR AZIZ: What kind of world have you in mind, Mr President, Mr Prime Minister, Mr Secretary-General, what kind of world do you work to preserve, where a mere 20 per cent on your side of this tiny planet take and hold and consume a full 80 per cent of its bounty? Tell me, please. I would know this. I would know this . . .

VOICE: (*Name*) Nidal.

(*She looks down again at the charcoal figure.*)

DR AZIZ: Qassem. Nidal. Four years one month. Hard of hearing. I will pray to my God for you, child. (*She looks up again.*) And what will you say to yours? No no no, please, this will not be justified by invoking the evil of my rulers or the unavoidability of your 'collateral damage', gentlemen. This world is full of evil rule, look at those you bought or bribed or bullied to give you houseroom here, look at those you would restore to their thrones, and tell me how we are worse. As for the unavoidable, how stupid, how very stupid you must think us, to imagine a decent human being believing you for one second, when you have told us and you have shown us your ability to tell the time on a child's wristwatch from one hundred miles, the side a woman parts her hair, the stubble on a man's face. We have a holy place, a place of worship, a place your cameras tell every day is filled with children. And you send a missile, not a wayward falling bomb, to burn it up . . . In the name of God? In the name of humankind? In the name of . . .

A FINAL VOICE: Suad.

(*She stands, gathers the charcoal sculpting in her hands, holds it to her face to kiss it.*)

DR AZIZ: Jubeh. Suad. Three. Arab. How can it matter? Yes. Not quite . . . one of you. Arab. Yes. But when the mouth

49

takes the nipple, the womb shivers just the same. (*Silence.*)
Gentle. Men.
(*She peers around the space.* RYDER *looks away.* O'TOOLE *sits on, retruded, scarcely there.* ISMAEL *stares out at the perimeter.*)
(*In Arabic*) You knew? Are you mad?
ISMAEL (*Not looking; in Arabic*) I had my orders.
DR AZIZ: (*Slow; in English*) So did they. They had their orders too . . .
(ISMAEL *calls to the perimeter, harsh, certain.* DR AZIZ *looks around her, as if dazed.* CHATTERJEE *climbs down from the scaffold, approaches her, a basket in his hand.*
She stares at it for some moments, kneels, places the bundle preciously inside.)
Call the mothers. Let them bury their own . . . Tell them to take comfort. In time we may come to see these as the lucky ones.
(CHATTERJEE *nods. The two heavies sent to drive her away arrive on the hulk; glare balefully at the problem woman. They part as she begins to leave, to let her through; follow her.*
O'TOOLE *stands. Sniffs, face satanic in the bloodied light.*
RYDER *edges towards the basket in* CHATTERJEE's *hands. A siren sounds, five miles away east.*)
RYDER: (*To whomever*) What we gonna do about this, then?
(*Silence.* ISMAEL *turns quietly, face deathly, pistol in hand.*)
ISMAEL: (*Deliberate*) You put it back. Is what you do. You put it back. Major's orders.
RYDER: (*Slow*) Hey, hang on a minute, friend . . .
O'TOOLE: (*In time*) Here, give it here.
(*He takes the basket from* CHATTERJEE, *leads them back to the wall, casually replaces the basket inside the shrine.*)
Wall party, fall in, let's go, it's time we were out of here . . .
(*He pushes* RYDER *up the steps;* RYDER's *legs have gone,* CHATTERJEE *has to help from above.* O'TOOLE *begins swinging blocks up to the platform.*
Distant explosions, five miles east.
Another siren sets up, a mile closer.
O'TOOLE *and* ISMAEL *check watches, as one.* ISMAEL *moves up to the rubble ridge, face blank, eyes bleak.*)

RYDER: (*Finding trowel; a sleepwalker*) I'm gonna make it. On my own, thank you. I've got a ticket, I've got a visa . . .

O'TOOLE: (*Casual, as he works*) Finish, leave, OK? The time for finesse is long past. Stay well away from miladdo, it's possible he's reached the end of his elastic . . .

RYDER: (*Laying*) I'm all right, I'm all right . . . Ticket, passport, visa.

O'TOOLE: OK. (*He dips into his bag, comes out with spray-can and lens-crown.*) Let's see if I can remember how this goes . . .

RYDER: You won't see me for dust . . . Ticket, pass . . .

O'TOOLE: Billy.

RYDER: Fuck off.

O'TOOLE: The papers, Billy.

RYDER: What about 'em?

O'TOOLE: (*Patient*) They're not. Chat'll tell you. Tell him, Chat. (*He pads off towards the pool.*)

RYDER: (*After him*) 'S he gonna do, drop me a line, he 's a dummy, right . . .? (*To* CHATTERJEE, *over shoulder*) Sorry, no offence intended . . .

CHATTERJEE: (*Own voice, Chapeltown*) None taken, don't mention it.

RYDER: (*After* O'TOOLE) Prick.
(*He swivels suddenly to look at* CHATTERJEE, *who's removing* RYDER's *papers from the envelope. He gropes in his pocket.*) Wait a minute . . .

CHATTERJEE: Bad news, friend.

RYDER: (*Snatching it*) Joke over, sunbeam.

CHATTERJEE: (*Resuming work*) Not if you try an' use that lot, pal. Your ticket'll get you in half-price at the Museum of the Arab on Hakawati, an' your visa's a menu from the Desert Bloom, a local chophouse . . .
(RYDER *lays grimly on, trying not to listen.*)
I've bin a coupla times, s'quite good.

RYDER: (*A mutter*) Two of a fuckin' kind, eh, a Paddy 'n' a Paki, just my luck . . .
(*A siren sets up, a mile closer.*
O'TOOLE *has knelt at the pool to wash: feet, torso, face and head. The washing is thorough, measured, flecks of ritual here*

and there about his process, focus inward throughout.
The Ancients rise up on the far side of the ridge, stand in silence to
watch the sun sinking beyond the city. On the siren, just set up,
they make a long, slow, unflurried exit.
ISMAEL stands suddenly, calls down to the men's perimeter; no
answer. He tries the women's; someone replies, voice edgy.
ISMAEL summons him up to the site. Truck doors slam, ignition,
the 5-tonner grinds away from the men's perimeter.)

O'TOOLE: (*Quiet; drying himself*) Exit the Guards.

(*He turns his head, gazes over at the scaffold.* CHATTERJEE's
trowel glints a signal: two rows.
The summoned guard appears at the hulk. He's fifteen; scared.
Explosions, a mile closer. The boy flinches.)

ISMAEL: (*In Arabic*) Who's left?

BOY: (*In Arabic*) Just me, sir.

(*ISMAEL nods gravely, takes the boy's Sten, orders him to the*
shelters. Turns. Scans the site. RYDER *and* CHATTERJEE *press*
on in silence, rhythm found again. O'TOOLE *has put on his*
lens-crown, fitted a fine-air nozzle to a paint can, begun test work
on a patch of masonry amid the rubble. ISMAEL *moves silently up*
behind him to watch.
Siren sounds, the other side of the city. Cuts. Deep silence.)

ISMAEL: O'Toole.

O'TOOLE: (*Absorbed*) Ismael.

ISMAEL: I phone my Major.

O'TOOLE: (*Working on*) What's he say?

ISMAEL: He say you know too much.

O'TOOLE: Ahunh.

(*ISMAEL looks across at the shrine.*)

ISMAEL: He say I have to kill you.

(*Silence.* O'TOOLE *works on, deep in process.*)

O'TOOLE: Did he say. Who he'd told. To kill you?

(*Explosions, far side of the city, intense, intermittent. Pricks of*
light pierce the gloom of the site. O'TOOLE *stands, wipes his*
hands, stares out. Distant fires begin to ruddy their faces.
A final deadly barrage. Silence.)

Rumours. Dreams. Superstitions. Tattle. Women's talk. A
hawk hovering above the shrine, dogs braying like donkeys,

headless horses in the souk, an empty school bus being
pushed into the river this morning, a driver shot, military
using the crèche at night, a mute who sang at sunset . . .
(CHATTERJEE's *voice floats out across the site, grave, slow, pure:*
'*Here we go, here we go, here we go* . . .'
The two men stare at each other in the near-dark.)
(*The wall*) All done, son.
(ISMAEL *frowns, peers across at the finished wall. The men have
gone.* ISMAEL *smiles, oddly.*)

ISMAEL: You fulla tricks, Gilderman.

O'TOOLE: We're all fulla someat. With you it's shit. You didn't
even know the babs were in there, did you, your Major told
you they'd been washed away in the river, he had you
execute the poor bloody driver for falling asleep at the wheel,
he fed you the cover story, you couldn't swallow it fast
enough, you took his lies for truth and now you're down to
die for it, you poor ignorant bastard . . .
(*Siren, sudden, loud, their sector. Neither moves. Siren cuts.
Silence.*)
(*Eventually; a whisper*) Let's go.
(*Silence.* ISMAEL *unslings the Sten from his shoulder. Stares at
it. Drops it into the pool. Draws his revolver carefully; it follows
the Sten. Stares up at the sky.*)

ISMAEL: I die is my business. Fuck off.
(O'TOOLE *smiles faintly, holds his hand out, palm up. Opens the
hand. Shows* ISMAEL *his bullets. They follow the weapons.*)

O'TOOLE: Go home, eh?

ISMAEL: You wanna go? Bye bye. Sure thing. I stay.
(O'TOOLE *shakes his head, gathers spray-can, walks slowly over
towards the shrine.*)

O'TOOLE: I'll go when I'm done.
(O'TOOLE *clambers up the scaffold, begins to work unseen on the
breezeblock wall.*
ISMAEL *watches him. Begins to laugh. Finds the ball. Flicks it
from foot to foot for a moment, then belts it into the blackness.*)

ISMAEL: (*Released; laughing; sobs*) You think you big man,
O'Toole? Tough guy, hunh? You think you better than
Ismael, eh? FUCK YOU, MISTER. (*Gathers bag, crosses to*

shrine.) DID ISMAEL DO THIS? EH? YOU THINK ISMAEL DID
THIS? YOU THINK MY MAJOR DID IT? YOU. YOU DID IT.
YOU NO GOOD. YOU NEVER NO GOOD. EVIL. EVIL.
(*He's wrenched the Man United shirt out, scrunches it to a ball,
throws it at the scaffold.* O'TOOLE *works on.*) You take. I don't
want this. You not fit to kiss my Major's arseholes, my
Major's a good man, three wars, an eye gone to the Jews, an
arm left in Persia, EVERY WEEK HE GIVE ME FREE TIME FOR
TRAINING . . . (*Sobs, fury, pain*) You people did this thing
. . . I not speak your words no more. (*His fingers tear at his
tongue*.) YOU DON'T JUDGE ISMAEL. NOT YOU PEOPLE. NOT
YOU PEOPLE . . .

(O'TOOLE'*s finished, lowers himself carefully down.* ISMAEL
*hurls himself up the ridge, falls to his knees, repeats fragments of
the outburst in Arabic.* O'TOOLE *moves some paces towards him.
Watches his hopeless weeping misery.
Bombs and missiles hit the sector with deafening abruptness, close
enough to feel the breath.* ISMAEL *looks up at the sky, arms lifted
as if in prayer*.)

(*In Arabic*) Ismael, son of Akram, brother of Saïd, spits in
your face, you Mongols, you hear me? You hear me?
Mongols . . .

(*Sound cuts. An extraordinary explosive light rips across the site.
Invisible cluster-bomb fragments follow its path, rip* ISMAEL
*along with them like a shirt on a line.
The blast passes. What's left of the young minder flops on its back
on the rubble slope. Smoke rises from a heap of clothing by the
shrine, all that's left of* O'TOOLE.
Distant rumbles. Silence.

CHATTERJEE *appears under the roof awning. He scans the
gloom, listens, swings lithely down, crosses to the ridge, gazes
mutely on* ISMAEL'*s remains, then goes to stand over* O'TOOLE'*s
mounded garb, lips pursed.
Sniffs. Gathers* O'TOOLE'*s grip and instrument case, finds the
lens-crown, puts it carefully on his head, takes a fallen lamp,
pads forward, gradually assumes the full* O'TOOLE *gesture*.)

CHATTERJEE: (*Lamp to face*) Now praise and glory be to Him who
sits throned in eternity above the shifts of time; who . . .

54

RYDER: (*Off, close; slow, soft, sung*) 'I've got a ticket to ride and I'm OK.'
(CHATTERJEE *looks around him. Siren sets up: all clear.* RYDER *emerges from shrine-side canvas, hands and knees.*)
I'm fine. I'm fine. Thanks.
(*The siren cuts. He stands. Pats breast pocket.*)
I'd like to go home now. If that could be arranged. I have the necessary . . . (*Holds up envelope.*) Ticket visa passport. A prile of priles. 138,000 quid in bank loans, me house, wife and business down the Swanee . . . Last time I vote bloody whatsit . . . (*Scans the site.*) Where's erm? (*Long silence.*) What are you, RAF? Pilot, yes? Half a million a year t'train you, 'course they're gonna send someone in. Brilliant. A mute called Chatty. Brilliant, both o' you. (*Silence.*) I was so scared. I was so . . . (*He shakes his head, turns, begins to leave.*) Bus station.
CHATTERJEE: (*Soft*) Billy.
RYDER: Can't hear you, sorry.
CHATTERJEE: Just wait by the corner, I'll take you down to the river, Persian steamer, gotta tidy up, I'll see you right. OK . . .?
RYDER: (*Turning*) Your oppo, what's-his-name, he could've had us all dead.
CHATTERJEE: Some of us are, Billy.
(*He swings his lamp across the dead* ISMAEL. RYDER *peers at it across the site.*)
RYDER: I meant us. I meant me.
(*He leaves.* CHATTERJEE *watches. Resumes.*)
CHATTERJEE: (*Lamp to face, master again*) . . . who, changing all things, remains himself unchanged; who alone is the paragon of all perfection . . .
(*A waking groan cuts him off.* O'TOOLE *stretches upward to sit on the crest of the rubble ridge. Blinks across at the Indian.* CHATTERJEE *shakes his head in disbelief.*)
O'TOOLE: You woke me up with your yammering. I was takin' a nap.
(*He looks around him, slowly reconnects, draws himself to his feet, sees the lens-crown.*)

Hey, don't get ahead o' yourself, you're a cheeky bugger . . .
Where's er . . .?

CHATTERJEE: Standin' by . . .

O'TOOLE: Best get after him, he'll be climbin' lamp-posts . . . I'll
see you down there, gotta tidy up . . . Java, here we come,
eh?

CHATTERJEE: (*Laying crown in* O'TOOLE's *bag*) Sod Java. Sod
you. I'm off back 'ome, look for someat on me own.

O'TOOLE: I got you out, didn't I? Some thanks.

CHATTERJEE: You got me bloody in too, O'Toole. Was you did
the gold tooth, when they came for you, you bloody shopped
me . . .

O'TOOLE: Grow up, boy. How in God's name were *you* gonna get
me out? Mm? You haven't the wit, son. When I took you on,
you were nobbut a scruffy lad labouring for a brickie at the
Harrogate Pump Room, I've shown you a true craft, I've
shown you the world according to O'Toole . . .

CHATTERJEE: Christ, what a clown. A legend in your own three-
ring circus . . . Come on, you bollox, let's go.

O'TOOLE: (*Sudden, hard*) I'm not done. Get off.

CHATTERJEE: (*Soft; unafraid*) I'll wait down the hill. You'll not
find your way else.

(*A final flurry of bombs and missiles rips into the city, a mile
away.*

CHATTERJEE *leaves.*

O'TOOLE *picks up his grip, slings instrument case, scans the site.
Takes in the dead* ISMAEL. *Gathers the Man United shirt from
the scaffolding. Carries it to the body. Crouches to gaze on the
stilled face.*)

O'TOOLE: Lord, hear my tale, and let my tale come unto thee.
Concerning young Ismael, the life to the death, a tragedy, if
you'll pardon the expression. Who, acting on orders, almost
single-handed, for a whole day kept the site of heinous and
hydra-headed infanticide under wraps until the evidence
could be buried and a covering account set in place by his
commander. Who failed to return from the brothel one
afternoon, and was not on hand when the crèche supervisor
rang in to say the bus had not arrived to take the kids over

the river. Who were simply left there, forgotten. In a building the military had begun using, with some sort of command 'n' control gear in the roof, a known target of enemy guided-fire since Day One. What a pickle. I pass over the part taken by the enemy, Lord, I know you're a sceptic on the matter. Save to ask whatever happened to proportion, doesn't this sort of thing stretch the credulity a touch, even yours, they could see it was being used for military purposes but managed to overlook – or at least overcome – the fact that it was in regular use as a *nursery*, oh come on, Lord, these men know *exactly* what they're doing, the rest is teasing. This boy, our hero, Lord, met death from a surfeit of orders and choked on his own obedience, for he was a good soldier . . .

(*He lays the shirt across the young man's face and body.* MAN UNITED *gleams up out of the gloom.*

He stands with effort. Looks up at the sky, out front.)

Finished?

(*No answer.*

What light's left begins to die. O'TOOLE *treads along the rubble ridge, fades into the dark.*

The gilder's lamp shines down on the face of the patched wall. The gilder's work shimmers strangely in the air, in front of rather than upon it. It reads, in English and Arabic, GOD IS GOOD, *under the image of a child's hand.*

Slow fade.

Dog breath.

The tent falls away; the building within shimmers in the dark. Points of fire begin to light the distant horizon. Hell reinvents itself. The world burns.

Western voices move in, out, on the fade, recounting the war they had.

The Ancients rise up from the rubble ridge. Stand, immutable, inerasable, staring out at the city.)